♑   THE CAPRICORN ENIGMA   ♑

Cracking the Code

ALSO BY JANE RIDDER-PATRICK

A Handbook of Medical Astrology
Shaping Your Future (Series of 12 titles)
Shaping Your Relationships (Series of 12 titles)

The Zodiac Code series

THE
CAPRICORN
ENIGMA

Cracking the Code

JANE RIDDER-PATRICK

MAINSTREAM
PUBLISHING
EDINBURGH AND LONDON

For Caro

First published in Great Britain in 2004 by
MAINSTREAM PUBLISHING COMPANY
(EDINBURGH) LTD
7 Albany Street
Edinburgh EH1 3UG

ISBN 1 84018 534 1

A catalogue record for this book is available
from the British Library

Typeset in Allise and Van Dijck

Printed in Great Britain by
Cox & Wyman Ltd

Contents

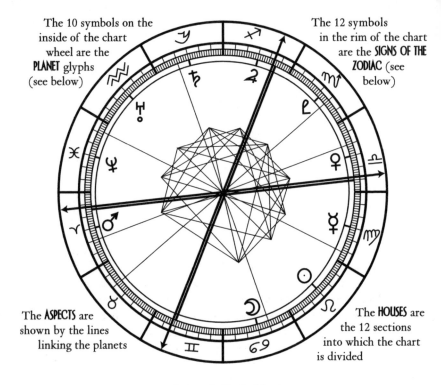

The 10 symbols on the inside of the chart wheel are the **PLANET** glyphs (see below)

The 12 symbols in the rim of the chart are the **SIGNS OF THE ZODIAC** (see below)

The **ASPECTS** are shown by the lines linking the planets

The **HOUSES** are the 12 sections into which the chart is divided

A Sample Birth Chart

Sign	Ruler	Sign	Ruler
Aries ♈	Mars ♂	Libra ♎	Venus ♀
Taurus ♉	Venus ♀	Scorpio ♏	Pluto ♇
Gemini ♊	Mercury ☿	Sagittarius ♐	Jupiter ♃
Cancer ♋	Moon ☽	Capricorn ♑	Saturn ♄
Leo ♌	Sun ☉	Aquarius ♒	Uranus ♅
Virgo ♍	Mercury ☿	Pisces ♓	Neptune ♆

ONE

The Truth of Astrology

MOST PEOPLE'S FIRST EXPERIENCE OF ASTROLOGY IS THROUGH newspapers and magazines. This is a mixed blessing for astrology's reputation – writing an astrology column to any degree of accuracy is a tough, many would say impossible, challenge. The astrologer has to try to say something meaningful about conditions that affect every single person belonging to the same sign, over a very short period of time, in a scant handful of words. The miracle is that some talented astrologers do manage to get across a tantalising whiff of the real thing and keep readers coming back for more of what most of us are hungry for – self-knowledge and reassurance about the future. The downside of the popularity of these columns is that many people think that all astrology is a branch of the entertainment industry and is limited to light-hearted fortune-telling. This is far from the truth.

What Astrology Can Offer

Serious astrology is one of the most sophisticated tools available to help us understand ourselves and the world around us. It gives us a language and a framework to examine and describe – quite literally – *anything* under the Sun, from countries to companies, from money markets to medical matters. Its most common application, however, is in helping people to understand themselves better using their own unique birth charts. Astrology has two main functions. One is to describe the traits and tendencies of whatever it is that is being examined, whether this is a state, a software company or someone's psyche. The other is to give an astonishingly accurate timetable for important changes within that entity. In the chapters that follow, we'll be using astrology to investigate the psychology of the innermost part of your personality, taking a look at what drives, inspires and motivates you.

Astrology uses an ancient system of symbols to describe profound truths about the nature of life on earth, truths that cannot be weighed and measured, but ones we recognise nevertheless, and that touch and move us at a deep level. By linking mythology and mathematics, astrology bridges the gap between our inner lives and our outer experiences, between mind and matter, between poetry and science.

Fate and Free Will

Some people think that astrology is all about foretelling the future, the implication being that everything is predestined and that we have no say in how our lives take shape. None of that is true. We are far from being helpless victims of fate. Everything that happens to us at any given time is the result of past choices. These choices may have been our own, or made by other people. They could even have been made long ago before we, or even our grandparents, were born. It is not always possible to prevent processes that were set in motion in the past from coming to their logical conclusions as events that we then have to deal with. We are, however, all free to decide how to react to whatever is presented to us at every moment of our lives.

Your destiny is linked directly with your personality because the choices you make, consciously or unconsciously, depend largely on your own natural inclinations. It is these inclinations that psychological astrology describes. You can live out every single part of your chart in a constructive or a less constructive way. For instance, if you have Aries strong in your chart, action and initiative will play a major role in your life. It is your choice whether you express yourself aggressively or assertively, heroically or selfishly, and also whether you are the doer or the done-to. Making the right choices is important because every decision has consequences – and what you give out, sooner or later, you get back. If you don't know and understand yourself, you are 'fated' to act according to instinct and how your life experiences have conditioned you. By revealing how you are wired up temperamentally, astrology can highlight alternatives to blind knee-jerk reactions, which often make existing problems worse. This self-knowledge can allow you to make more informed free-will choices, and so help you create a better and more successful future for yourself.

Astrology and Prediction

Astrology cannot predict specific events based on your birth chart. That kind of prediction belongs to clairvoyance and divination. These specialities, when practised by gifted and responsible individuals, can give penetrating insights into events that are likely to happen in the future if matters proceed along their present course.

The real benefit of seeing into the future is that if we

don't like what could happen if we carry on the way we're going, we can take steps either to prevent it or to lessen its impact. Rarely is the future chiselled out in stone. There are many possible futures. What you feed with your attention grows. Using your birth chart, a competent astrologer can map out, for years in advance, major turning points, showing which areas of your life will be affected at these times and the kind of change that will be taking place. This information gives answers to the questions that most clients ask in one way or another: 'Why me, why this and why now?' If you accept responsibility for facing what needs to be done at the appropriate time, and doing it, you can change the course of your life for the better.

Astrology and the Soul

What is sometimes called the soul and its purpose is a mystery much more profound than astrology. Most of us have experienced 'chance' meetings and apparent 'tragedies' which have affected the direction of our entire lives. There is an intelligence at work that is infinitely wiser and more powerful than the will or wishes of our small, egocentric personalities. This force, whatever name we give it – Universal Wisdom, the Inner Guide, the Self, a guardian angel – steers us into exactly the right conditions for our souls' growth. Astrology can pinpoint the turning points in the course of your destiny and describe the equipment that you have at your disposal for serving, or resisting, the soul's purpose. That equipment is your personality.

Who Are You?

You are no doubt aware of your many good qualities as well as your rather more resistible ones that you might prefer to keep firmly under wraps. Maybe you have wondered why it is that one part of your personality seems to want to do one thing while another part is stubbornly intent on doing the exact opposite. Have you ever wished that you could crack the code that holds the secrets of what makes you – and significant others – behave in the complex way you do? The good news is that you can, with the help of your astrological birth chart, sometimes known as your horoscope.

Just as surely as your DNA identifies you and distinguishes you from everyone else, as well as encoding your peculiarities and potential, your birth chart reveals the unique 'DNA fingerprinting' of your personality. This may seem a staggering claim, but it is one that those who have experienced serious astrology will endorse, so let's take a closer look at what a birth chart is.

Your Birth Chart

Your birth chart is a simplified diagram of the positions of the planets, as seen from the place of your birth, at the moment you took your first independent breath. Critics have said that astrology is obviously nonsense because birth charts are drawn up as if the Sun and all the planets move round the Earth.

We know in our minds that the Earth moves round the Sun, but that doesn't stop us seeing the Sun rise in the east in the morning and move across the sky to set in the west in the evening. This is an optical illusion. In the same way, we know (or at least most of us know) that we are not really the centre of the universe, but that doesn't stop us experiencing ourselves as being at the focal point of our own personal worlds. It is impossible to live life in any other way. It is the strength, not weakness, of astrology that it describes from your own unique viewpoint how you, as an individual, experience life.

Erecting Your Chart

To draw up a full birth chart you need three pieces of information – the date, time and place of your birth. With your birth date alone you can find the positions of all the planets (except sometimes the Moon) to a good enough degree of accuracy to reveal a great deal of important information about you. If you have the time and place of birth, too, an astrologer can calculate your Ascendant or Rising Sign and the houses of your chart – see below. The Ascendant is a bit like the front door of your personality and describes your general outlook on life. (If you know your Ascendant sign, you might like to read more about its characteristics in the book on that sign in this series.)

The diagram on page 6 shows what a birth chart looks like. Most people find it pretty daunting at first sight but it actually breaks down into only four basic units – the planets, the signs, the aspects and the houses.

The Planets

Below is a simple list of what the planets represent.

PLANET	REPRESENTS YOUR URGE TO
☉ The Sun	express your identity
☽ The Moon	feel nurtured and safe
☿ Mercury	make connections
♀ Venus	attract what you love
♂ Mars	assert your will
♃ Jupiter	find meaning in life
♄ Saturn	achieve your ambitions
♅ Uranus	challenge tradition
♆ Neptune	serve an ideal
♇ Pluto	eliminate, transform and survive

The planets represent the main psychological drives that every single one of us has. The exact way in which we express these drives is not fixed from birth but develops and evolves throughout our lives, both consciously and unconsciously. In this book we will be examining in detail four of these planets – your Sun, Moon, Mercury and Venus. These are the bodies that are right at the heart of our solar system. They correspond, in psychological astrology, to the core of your personality and represent how you express yourself, what motivates you emotionally, how you use your mind and what brings you pleasure.

The Signs

The signs your planets are in show how you tend to express your inner drives. For example, if your Mars is in the action sign of Aries, you will assert yourself pretty directly, pulling no punches. If your Venus is in secretive Scorpio, you will attract, and also be attracted to, emotionally intense relationships. There is a summary of all of the signs on p. 128.

The Aspects

Aspects are important relationships between planets and whether your inner characteristics clash with or complement each other depends largely on whether or not they are in aspect and whether that aspect is an easy or a challenging one. In Chapter Six we'll be looking at some challenging aspects to the Sun.

The Houses

Your birth chart is divided into 12 slices, called houses, each of which is associated with a particular area of life, such as friendships, travel or home life. If, for example, you have your Uranus in the house of career, you are almost certainly a bit of a maverick at work. If you have your Neptune in the house of partnership, you are likely to idealise your husband, wife or business partner.

The Nature of Time

Your birth chart records a moment in time and space, like a still from a movie – the movie being the apparent movement of the planets round the earth. We all know that time is something that can be measured in precise units, which are always the same, like seconds, months and centuries. But if you stop to reflect for a moment, you'll also recognise that time doesn't always feel the same. Twenty minutes waiting for a bus on a cold, rainy day can seem like a miserable eternity, while the same amount of time spent with someone you love can pass in a flash. As Einstein would say – that's relativity.

There are times in history when something significant seems to be in the air, but even when nothing momentous is happening the quality of time shifts into different 'moods' from moment to moment. Your birth chart is impregnated with the qualities of the time when you were born. For example, people who were born in the mid-to-late 1960s, when society was undergoing major disruptive changes, carry those powerful energies within them and their personalities reflect, in many ways, the turmoil of those troubled and exciting times. Now, as adults, the choices that those individuals make, based on their own inner conflicts and compulsions, will help shape the future of society for better or worse. And so it goes on through the generations.

Seed Meets Soil

There is no such thing as a good or bad chart, nor is any one sign better or worse than another. There are simply 12 different, but equally important, life focuses. It's useful to keep in mind the fact that the chart of each one of us is made up of all the signs of the zodiac. This means that we'll act out, or experience, *every* sign somewhere in our lives. It is true, however, that some individual charts are more challenging than others; but the greater the challenge, the greater the potential for achievement and self-understanding.

In gardening terms, your chart is a bit like the picture on a seed packet. It shows what you could become. If the seeds are of poppies, there's no way you'll get petunias, but external conditions will affect how they grow. With healthy soil, a friendly climate and green-fingered gardeners, the plants have an excellent chance of flourishing. With poor soil, a harsh climate or constant neglect, the seeds will be forced to struggle. This is not always a disadvantage. They can become hardy and adapt, finding new and creative ways of evolving and thriving under more extreme conditions than the plant that was well cared for. It's the same with your chart. The environment you were raised in may have been friendly or hostile to your nature and it will have done much to shape your life until now. Using the insights of astrology to affirm who you are, you can, as an adult, provide your own ideal conditions, become your own best gardener and live out more fully – and successfully – your own highest potential.

TWO

The Symbolism of Capricorn

WE CAN LEARN A GREAT DEAL ABOUT CAPRICORN BY looking at the symbolism and the myths and legends associated with it. These carry more information than plain facts alone and hint at the deeper meanings and significance of the sign.

The Capricorn glyph of a V-shape joined to a swirling half-circle has been interpreted in many ways over the years. It has been seen as the joint of the knee, which Capricorn rules. When the knee is inflexible and unbending, a person can only move forward slowly and awkwardly, if at all. Kneeling, as well as curtseying, are signs of recognising and serving a higher authority. It is also the usual position for prayer. Capricorns are eager to have the status and recognition of their rank, but until they learn humility, and to acknowledge and submit their will to something higher than themselves, they cannot reach their full potential as responsible leaders of their communities. Most commonly the left half of the glyph has been seen as the hard, angular head and horn of a goat and the rest as a curving fish-tail. This seems a strange coupling, but a closer examination of Capricorn's symbol will shed some light on the mystery.

Capricorn the Goat

Capricorn's symbol is the goat and these come in several varieties. There is the domestic goat; this is kept tethered to a post by a short rope and is milked regularly. It rarely escapes from its own backyard and if it does, is soon brought back, and chastised firmly, after a few hours of freedom savouring titbits from neighbouring washing lines. If you are a domestic-goat Capricorn, you may feel that your life is one unending round of duty with little prospect of being let off the hook until retirement. The mountain goat, on the other hand, is going places. It may look ill-equipped to scale the heights but it is patient and skilled at perching on perilous places with very little foothold. Each step has to be calculated carefully or it could take a tumble, but slowly, and increasingly surely, it climbs upwards, every move bringing it closer to the summit, where it will be master of all it surveys. This kind of goat has the patience and self-control to wait until the time and conditions are right. If you are one of these, you are almost certain to succeed, but may be so focused on your own ambitions that you forget to enjoy the flowers and the balmy breezes on the way up – or worse, ignore, snub or trample over those you overtake – and live to regret it on the way back down.

The older Capricorn symbol is the Sea Goat – also called the Mer-Goat – which is a goat with a fish-tail where the hind legs should be. It knows the secrets of worldly affairs but also understands that the source of real power and wealth is beyond the ego. This goat wants to put its wisdom, and all the Earth's resources, to serve the good of humanity. It is sensitive to both its own needs and the needs of those in its circle of influence, and gladly works away quietly, often behind the scenes, to create responsible organisations and regulatory structures to ensure that order and justice prevail in society. If you are a Sea Goat, you can truly help create peace and plenty on earth.

The Ruler of Capricorn

Each sign is associated with a planet called its ruler. Saturn, ruler of Capricorn, was the incorruptible Roman god of fertility, agriculture and abundance, who presided over the golden age when gods and humans worked together harmoniously. At that time there were neither wars nor hardships. Saturn is sometimes called the Lord of Karma, referring to the fact that we reap what we sow – something that Capricorns are usually well aware of.

The Greek name for Saturn was Cronus. He is often shown carrying a sickle showing his connection with harvesting the riches of the earth. It also refers to the story of him castrating his tyrannical father, Uranus, with a sickle, then ruling in his place. Unfortunately Cronus became a tyrant, too, and in time was overthrown by his own son, Zeus. Modern versions of Cronus are Old Father Time and the Grim Reaper, the skeleton with the sickle, who rules time and death. These stories illustrate the two paths that you can take as a Capricorn. One way leads to honour and riches through honesty and hard work, the other to trouble and tyranny through being overbearing and over-ambitious.

Capricorn in Myth and Legend

The lusty shepherd god Pan, with hairy goat's legs, is also associated with Capricorn. During a war between the gods and titans, the gods were driven into Egypt. To escape from harm, each of the gods had to change shape. Pan jumped into the Nile and changed the upper part of his body into a goat and lower into a fish. Pan's name means 'he who feeds' and in Latin the word 'panis' means bread; appropriate indeed for Capricorn's role, which is often as provider and breadwinner. Pan used to beat his enemies by infecting them with an irrational fear or 'panic'. Some Capricorns can be equally terrifying, while others get into irrational panics themselves when overwhelmed by fear of the disapproval of their superiors.

The Season of Capricorn

The Sun enters Capricorn at the winter solstice when, in the northern hemisphere, the days begin to lengthen and the light is returning, which is why, in Christianity, the birth of Christ, the light of the world, is celebrated at this time. An earlier Roman festival for Saturn, called Saturnalia, was held at mid-winter, when all business was suspended and masters waited on their slaves. Winter now begins in earnest and on New Year's Day it is customary to look forward to the coming year and make resolutions, which rarely last – unless you are a disciplined Capricorn, of course. January is named after Janus, the Roman god of doors and beginnings. With his two heads, he looks both forward and back, just like Capricorns who are both ambitious for the future and respectful of the past. Beginnings are seen as crucial to the success of any undertaking and they are gateways to the future. Wise Capricorns are well aware of that and so are astrologers who are interested in politics and business affairs. They cast horoscopes, set for the various places on earth, for the moment the Sun enters Capricorn each year to get an idea of the influences that will affect the world in general, and their own locality in particular, over the coming year.

THREE

The Heart of the Sun

O THE GLYPH FOR THE SUN IS A PERFECT CIRCLE WITH A DOT in the centre and symbolises our dual nature — earthly and eternal. The circle stands for the boundary of the personality, which distinguishes and separates each individual from every other individual, for it is our differences from other people that make us unique, not our similarities. The dot in the centre indicates the mysterious 'divine spark' within us and the potential for becoming conscious of who we truly are, where we have come from and what we may become.

The Meaning of the Sun
Each of your planets represents a different strand of your personality. The Sun is often reckoned to be the most important factor of your whole birth chart. It describes your sense of identity, and the sign that the Sun was in when you were born, your Sun sign, along with its house position and any aspects to other planets, shows how you express and develop that identity.

Your Role in Life

Each of the signs is associated with certain roles that can be played in an infinite number of ways. Take one of the roles of Aries, which is the warrior. A warrior can cover anything from Attila the Hun, who devastated vast stretches of Europe with his deliberate violence, to an eco-warrior, battling to save the environment. The role, warrior, is the same; the motivation and actions are totally different. You can live out every part of your personality in four main ways – as creator, destroyer, onlooker or victim. How you act depends on who you choose to be from the endless variations possible from the symbolism of each of your planets, but most particularly your Sun. And you do have a choice; not all Geminis are irresponsible space cadets nor is every Scorpio a sex-crazed sadist. This book aims to paint a picture of what some of your choices might be and show what choices, conscious or unconscious, some well-known people of your sign have made.

Your upbringing will have helped shape what you believe about yourself and out of those beliefs comes, automatically, behaviour to match. For example, if you believe you are a victim, you will behave like one and the world will happily oblige by victimising you. If you see yourself as a carer, life will present you with plenty to care for – and often to care about, too. If you identify yourself as an adventurer, you'll spot opportunities at every corner. If you're a winner, then you'll tend to succeed. Shift the way that you see yourself and your whole world shifts, too.

Your Vocation

Your Sun describes your major life focus. This is not always a career. As the poet Milton said: 'They also serve who only stand and wait.' It is impossible to tell from your Sun sign exactly what your calling is – there are people of all signs occupied in practically every area of life. What is important is not so much *what* you do, but the way that you do it and it is this – how you express yourself – that your Sun describes. If you spend most of your time working at an occupation or living in a situation where you can't give expression to the qualities of your Sun, or which forces you to go against the grain of your Sun's natural inclinations, then you're likely to live a life of quiet, or possibly even noisy, desperation.

On Whose Authority

Your personality, which your birth chart maps, is like a sensitive instrument that will resonate only to certain frequencies – those that are similar to its own. Your Sun shows the kind of authority that will strike a chord with you, either positively or negatively, because it is in harmony with yours. It can show how you relate to people in authority, especially your father. (It is the Moon that usually shows the relationship with your mother and home.) In adult life it can throw light onto the types of bosses you are likely to come across, and also how you could react to them. It is a major part of the maturing process to take responsibility for expressing your own authority wisely. When you do so, many of your problems with external authorities diminish or even disappear.

In a woman's chart the Sun can also describe the kind of husband she chooses. This is partly because, traditionally, a husband had legal authority over his wife. It is also because, especially in the early years of a marriage, many women choose to pour their energies into homemaking and supporting their husbands' work in the world, rather than their own, and so his career becomes her career. As a

Capricorn, you may find that your father, boss or husband shows either the positive or negative traits of Capricorn or, as is usually the case, a mixture of both – responsible, hard-working and disciplined or dictatorial, cold and miserly.

Born on the Cusp

If you were born near the beginning or end of Capricorn, you may know that your birthday falls on the cusp, or meeting point, of two signs. The Sun, however, can only be in one sign or the other. You can find out for sure which sign your Sun is in by checking the tables on pp.96–7.

FOUR

The Drama of Being a Capricorn

EACH SIGN IS ASSOCIATED WITH A CLUSTER OF ROLES THAT HAVE their own core drama or storyline. Being born is a bit like arriving in the middle of an ongoing play and slipping into a certain part. How we play our characters is powerfully shaped in early life by having to respond to the input of the other actors around us – the people that make up our families and communities. As the play of our lives unfolds, we usually become aware that there are themes which tend to repeat themselves. We may ask ourselves questions like 'Why do I always end up with all the work / caught up in fights / with partners who mistreat me / in dead-end jobs / successful but unhappy . . .?' or whatever. Interestingly, I've found that people are less likely to question the wonderful things that happen to them again and again.

The good news is that once we recognise the way we have been playing our roles, we can then use our free-will choice to do some creative rescripting, using the same character in more constructive scenarios. Even better news is that if we change, the other people in our dramas have got to make some alterations, too. If you refuse to respond to the same old cues in the customary ways, they are going to have to get creative, too.

A key role of Capricorn is the manager. A manager is responsible for ensuring the smooth and efficient running of a company, organisation or system, which can be anything from a family to a country or a multinational corporation. Good managers must have a clear grasp of the long-term aims of their business so that they can direct all of their efforts, and that of the workforce, towards that end. They need to be able to draw up plans and strategies about how to get from where they are at the moment to where they want to be in one year's, five years' and ten years' time. Smart managers check out what has worked in the past in similar situations and apply that to good effect.

They need to attend to the details of day-to-day administration so that it is done effectively and people and parts move like well-oiled machinery. To help make sure that everyone knows where they are and is moving in the same direction, managers need to lay down ground rules, apply regulations and set up an effective system of rewards and penalties to encourage workers to give of their best. The balance, however, must be right between the stick and the carrot: too severe and he or she turns into a tyrant and may be overthrown like the heads of the Cronus dynasty; too lax and the organisation will fall to pieces. A manager needs to have the strength of character, or a thick enough skin, to be able to bear being disliked for unpopular decisions and for temporary restrictions that will benefit the long-term goal. That means being able to stand alone.

On the way up, he or she needs to know how to take orders and please those in upper management while effectively directing those below. Insecure middle managers have been likened to people riding a bicycle, bending their backs and bowing their heads to those above while trampling like crazy on those below. Managers, like other workers, are at a certain stage ousted, either because they have reached retirement age or because they are displaced by younger and more ruthless candidates from the lower ranks – again, echoes of Cronus. Their wisdom, experience and expertise accumulated over the years, though, can be an invaluable resource and smart companies often call in retired managers as consultants.

Most Capricorns, at some time in their lives, go through a period of being trapped by responsibilities – welcome or unwelcome – like having to take over the family business, bringing up a child single-handedly or even just being plunged too early into adulthood when other children are still out playing. Some take on burdens willingly even though they may not need to, while others try to avoid duties and commitments as long as possible. One way or another, the day of reckoning does come when you are forced to face the reality, hardships and limitations of life in the flesh. Capricorn's drama includes heavy responsibilities but the rewards can be as rich as the road is hard. After all, it is heavy pressure over time that creates diamonds from dross.

Other Capricorn roles are the elder, high priest, supervisor, director, committee member and bureaucrat, all of which entail taking responsibility for large-scale, long-term projects that affect in some way the regulation and running of society.

How you choose to see your role will determine your behaviour. The following chapter describes some typical Capricorn behaviour. Remember, though, that there is no such thing as a person who is all Capricorn and nothing but Capricorn. You are much more complicated than that and other parts of your chart will modify, or may even seem to contradict, the single, but central, strand of your personality which is your Sun sign. These other sides of your nature will add colour and contrast and may restrict or reinforce your basic Capricorn identity. They won't, however, cancel out the challenges you face as a Capricorn.

FIVE

The Capricorn Temperament

A JOURNEY OF A THOUSAND MILES, ACCORDING TO AN OLD Chinese saying, begins with a single step. To reach the final destination, all that is required is to keep on putting one foot in front of the other, patiently negotiating every obstacle that lies in the way until finally, and inevitably, the goal is reached. This is the story of Capricorn's life. Another way of putting it, when yet another of those obstacles looms, is that life is just one damned thing after another. Your capacity to commit yourself fully, together with your patience and determination, ensures that whatever you set your sights on, given time, you've every chance of achieving it.

Delaying Gratification
You are prepared to suffer – and inflict – temporary hardships for the sake of future gains. As you're always thinking ahead, you're not afraid to tighten your belt and save now in order to be able to put down a deposit for a house or start your own business a year or two down the line. Your iron discipline can greatly benefit those under

you, too, though it might not feel like that to them at the time. You can be the kind of boss who demands perfect performance and timekeeping, or a parent who insists that homework always be done properly. While this can produce groans and resistance, many have cause to be grateful later as it equips them better for life.

Time, Please

Time is always an issue for earth signs, most especially Capricorns. There never seems to be enough of it. Being a responsibility magnet, hard work, as well as hard challenges, gravitate towards you and you may find yourself running on a treadmill to catch up with the ever-increasing number of tasks that accumulate. 'Time is money,' said Benjamin Franklin and wise Capricorns know that time is actually on their side. If you just keeping going in the same direction, and never, ever give up, success is bound to come your way. As Capricorn Louis Pasteur said: 'Let me tell you the secret that has led me to my goal. My strength lies in my tenacity.' Yours does, too.

Serious Concerns

Some Capricorns carry around with them an aura of earnestness, wearing their obligations like a sombre mantle, as if weighed down with care. Low-grade worry and fear of loss, which you can find hard to shake off, can be an almost permanent feature of your inner landscape. Even if the rest of your planets are in light-hearted, party-loving signs, you can be melancholic and solitary at times. When Edgar Allan Poe wrote his adult fairy tale 'The Raven', instead of the usual 'Once upon a time', he started it with the words 'Once upon a midnight dreary' because he said that's what this time always felt like.

Benjamin Franklin, intent on self-improvement, drew up a list of 13 virtues, focusing on one every week in turn. He originally had only 12 until someone pointed out that he was considered proud so, as an afterthought, he added 'Humility'. A friend of mine was told that playful spontaneity, a foreign concept for many Capricorns, was essential for a well-balanced life so she solemnly took out her organiser, sucked her pen thoughtfully while flicking through the pages, then entered 'plfl. spont.' every second Tuesday between 9.30 and 10.00 p.m.

Youth and Age

Many Capricorns appear to have been born old. How often were you told as a child that you acted and spoke like a little old grandma or grandpa? The bonus here is that, once you've served your time and made your way in the world, you are then free to start to develop your child-like sense of wonder and fun and rich sense of humour. Like many Capricorns, you've probably had more than your fair share of limitations and responsibilities in early years which frustrated your dreams and desires, leaving you, at times, depressed and lonely. But as you get older and more experienced, the reward is that you can turn these apparent adversities to your own advantage. Life has a way of sending blessings in curious disguises and, instead of becoming bitter, you may look back in gratitude at some of life's hard-earned lessons, and even smile at their ironical aptness, though you almost certainly wouldn't want to go through them again.

Scaling the Heights

You are at home in hierarchies, both at work and socially, where stages and ranks and official titles are clearly defined and you know your place and everyone else knows theirs, too. You have respect for those above you in the pecking order and would rarely think of disobeying them, and when you are in charge you expect obedience in return as your right. Because you're so focused on achievement, it's easy for you to be impressed by social and material success and to reject people who seem like losers or haven't much to contribute to your plans for getting ahead. Some Capricorns can be insensitive snobs who never see beyond appearances – to their own detriment, as well as those they snub.

Going Up

Capricorns are ambitious. You need a goal of some kind to aim at. It could be getting into the most prestigious golf club, being given the key to the executive lavatory or having your photo in *Tatler* or *Hello*. You may want to run a country, a nightclub, a sect, a corporation or a family dynasty, or, like Albert Schweitzer, build a leper hospital in Africa. It doesn't matter what you are aiming at, as long as it means something to you. A goat without a goal is a miserable, lost creature and can easily sink into depression and apathy. Once you're set on a target, you'll work relentlessly towards it, not being put off by even the most formidable obstructions in your way.

Behind the Mask

Your reputation is important to you and you take your public image very seriously indeed. You don't like your private affairs being pried into and anybody who tries to crowbar their way in is inviting a severe case of frostbite. You need to choose your public role carefully, one that expresses your own authentic values and interests, because if your personal and public lives don't mesh, you'll be deeply unhappy.

Snakes and Ladders

There is nothing more painful than putting your all into climbing a ladder and then finding out, 50 years later, that it was up against the wrong wall. Capricorns who use their talents for personal gain and self-aggrandisement can become materialistic, calculating, manipulative and power hungry, taking every unscrupulous opportunity to exploit the weak. Even if they manage to claw their way up, they tend to be empty, unsatisfied and desperately lonely when they reach the top. Capricorn gone wrong can be more sinister and sadistic than the dark side of Scorpio. The Capricorn dictator Stalin butchered millions of his own Russian countrymen; Hitler had his Moon in Capricorn and Dr Harold Shipman murdered over 200 of his elderly patients for reasons best known to himself. Mercifully, most Capricorns aim to become pillars of society and pour their dynamic energies into making substantial contributions to the community at large.

Rules and Regulations

Whatever your field, you like to be acquainted with its rules and regulations. Sometimes you can forget that what matters is the spirit of the law, not enforcing it to the letter. Most Capricorns are born with wagging index fingers. As far as you are concerned, a rule is a rule and any infringement, no matter how small, must be pointed out and the wrongdoer properly ticked off and punished. Orders are orders and you're rarely willing to discuss them with those you see as your subordinates – like the nineteenth-century German duke who hung a prominent notice in his estate office: 'Underlings are forbidden to apply the standards of their limited understanding to the dealings of their superiors.'

Most Capricorns are fond of abiding by traditional

rules, but if you feel overlooked or have had punishing parents, you could try to establish your own hierarchy with you as head of state. If anyone wants to bypass the laws of the land, and create their own, few do it better than Capricorns. It's interesting, however, that those who veer off the straight and narrow tend to come a cropper, like gangster Al Capone, who was eventually jailed for tax evasion, and US president Richard Nixon, who was caught telling Watergate whoppers in the White House.

Crime and Punishment

Your awareness of crime and punishment can make you prey to free-floating guilt, always looking over your shoulder for disapproval for offences you might unknowingly have committed yourself. Sometimes it is hard for you to admit you got it wrong. I have known Capricorns deny outright something they quite clearly did, because of the fear of consequences. Owning up to weakness or that you could do with some help is often difficult, too. It's important to lighten up: the more mercy and understanding you show towards others, the less emotionally insecure you'll feel yourself.

Traditional Values

You have a deep respect for time-honoured customs and the wisdom of the past. You probably know your family history inside out and may love antiques or visiting old buildings. You want to uphold tradition, and can sometimes idealise the past. Your real task is to bring the best of established values into the present so that you can build a secure future for those who come after you. The thought of leaving something behind to be remembered by gives you great pleasure and the idea of planting trees for posterity, even though you will never see them mature, could greatly appeal.

Cool Reception

You can be rather reserved and keep your real feelings buried deep, even if they are powerful. Think of the Queen, who has her Ascendant in Capricorn. Like you, she doesn't react with any great outer display of emotion, but prefers to stay cool and reticent. This can be hard for the more exuberant fire signs and heart-on-their-sleeves water people to understand. You, however, prefer to wait and see what develops before celebrating or commiserating too soon about events.

Far from always being a handicap, your ability to stay aloof and do your duty is an important asset, as your success may often depend on being equally unmoved by whether you are adored or disliked by those below. You tend to keep your distance and don't get too involved in other people's personal affairs, and can be masterfully oblivious to problems you don't want to deal with. This detachment allows you to operate independently. If you were too easily influenced by praise or blame, your long-term projects and plans would be quickly derailed. Yet you do need to pay attention to feelings, your own as well as others', while at the same time sticking to what your integrity tells you is right.

Calculating Capricorn

Unlike Sagittarians, who are perfectly happy to trust their luck, you leave nothing to chance and will rarely act impulsively. You'll work things out carefully first, scanning schemes for possible snags, and come up with a realistic strategy for achieving your aims. A few unscrupulous Capricorns use and abuse people like chess pieces to make their next few moves and then turn self-righteous in justifying to themselves that this is a necessary means to an end. It's scary for you to let go of the reins of control and to develop faith that life can be trusted. Like Benjamin

Franklin, you may believe that there is nothing certain in life but death and taxes, but you actually don't have to carry the weight of the world on your shoulders. That job, in case you hadn't noticed, has already been taken.

Rooted in Realism

Fantasy has little place in your life. You are a realist, especially about money. As Capricorn singer Sophie Tucker said: 'From birth to 18 a girl needs good parents. From 18 to 35, she needs good looks. From 35 to 55, good personality. From 55 on, she needs good cash. I'm saving my money.' You've an excellent money sense and, being economical and prudent, believe in saving for your retirement. You've very little time for waste, frivolity or flash. It's the control and security that money gives, rather than money itself, that matters to you.

While saving is important, you can spend lavishly if you believe it will improve your image and status; Capricorns who have reached the top can be generous in donating to charity and public works. You're not so much a hoarder like Taurus or Scorpio, preferring to move and use your money in buying and selling and trading. You drive a hard, but usually fair, bargain and you'll expect others to haggle just as hard with you. You reckon that people who get swindled have only themselves to blame for not checking all the angles the way you do.

Badges of Office

In order to feel worthwhile, you must have some achievement to show for your efforts, like property, position or even simply a duty that you have to fulfil. As you need approval, and to feel in control, you often can't bear to be bettered. When others talk about their successes, you could be tempted to turn to one-upmanship, implying condescendingly that your tennis club or antecedents or qualifications are just that bit better than theirs. When you learn to set your own standards and give yourself the approval, encouragement and respect you are due, you'll be free of the craving to have it from others.

Capricorn at Work

Capricorns are hard and responsible workers, prepared to beaver away from dawn to dusk if need be. You are best in a job where you can, slowly but surely, work your way up the ranks, accumulating position, status and security as you rise, as well as power and mastery over others. You like to have solid qualifications, preferably from the most respected and well-established institutions, as you feel safer with the rubber stamp of official approval backing you up. Working in the background, where the real power is, suits you – preferably behind a job title which underlines your status, but protects your privacy. You don't intend to stay in a lowly position for long but you are perfectly prepared to tug your forelock to your superiors if that's what it takes to get promotion. Having a place in, and making a contribution to, society and being recognised for your efforts matter as much, if not more, than financial rewards.

Choice Careers

Capricorn is the sign of the administrator, official and overseer. You might be happy working in a family business or a large corporation, or be drawn to politics or the civil service. Mathematics, science or the legal profession would satisfy your interest in the laws of society or nature. Working with the body, especially the bones and skin – like massage, aromatherapy and osteopathy – might also be a good career choice.

The Capricorn Boss

Male or female, you tend to be a bit of a father figure at work – a hard taskmaster but kindly when anyone is genuinely in need. You expect people to do as they're told, as democracy isn't a concept that you care for, though fairness is. Being conscientious and businesslike, you have the grit and tenacity to stick with any job through to the end. The only risks you will take are calculated ones and you intensely dislike delegating real responsibility. With your eyes wide open for the main chance, you want control and to be in a position of minimum risk with maximum gain.

If Capricorn women choose domesticity and don't go into business themselves, they can often be the driving force behind their husband's success – but God help the man who doesn't get on. It's often difficult for you to understand people who can't or won't get themselves sorted out and you've little time for slackers.

Capricorn and Health

Capricorn rules all of the body scaffolding and boundaries – the skin and bones, as well as the teeth and joints, especially the knees. Broken bones, sprains and dislocations are common among Capricorns, as are depression, arthritis and skin sensitivities, like rashes and allergies. When under stress, the thyroid gland can become overactive. Your teeth tend to be either one of your best features or a rich source of revenue for your dentist. If your knees cause problems, remember that psychologically the knees are related to humility and mortality, so addressing these issues may prove helpful.

You do, however, have some formidable health advantages on your side. There is your self-discipline, for a start. If you decide on a health regime, you usually have no problem in sticking to it, and your frugal habits are a major bonus. Your tendency to pessimism and worry – not to mention your workaholic tendencies – can undermine an otherwise excellent constitution. Developing a positive attitude in all circumstances and practising tolerance, both towards yourself and others, cultivating your rich sense of humour and learning to play and to enjoy all the success you've worked so hard to achieve can enhance the quality of your life. And who knows, it might even save it.

Capricorn Relating

Capricorns often have a great many associates but few close friends. To those whose loyalty has been tested and found true, you can be generous in the extreme. You would prefer to deprive yourself and take on extra burdens rather than let your loved ones suffer. Intimate relationships aren't always easy, as it can be hard for you to handle affection. Underneath that tough exterior, you've a soft, romantic, marshmallow core, but you've got to feel safe before you'll expose it. You long for freedom, adventure and romance but duty takes first place, even in love. When it comes to marriage, you tend to be as practical and serious as you are in other departments of life. Although you prefer to marry for love, you'll check out the credentials, pedigree and potential of any prospective partner before making a commitment. Capricorns rarely marry below their station and frequently above it. After all, why settle for the porter if there's a surgeon going spare? This all sounds rather chilly and more like a business deal than true love. Correct. Arranged marriages would have suited Capricorns perfectly, as you believe in getting the foundations laid first and letting love grow later, so long engagements are common.

A Capricorn woman is like a dream come true for a man who wants to get ahead, as she is supportive and ambitious – provided she doesn't have career goals of her own that clash with her partner's. Capricorn men tend to be rather traditional, seeing women as wives and mothers, and can feel threatened if their partners have a career, especially one that is more successful than their own. They like to be at the head of the table and in charge of family affairs. You want someone you can depend on and, once committed, you are loyal, responsible and utterly reliable. You are capable of great devotion and are willing to put a lot of effort and tolerance into making a relationship work. You believe a marriage should develop slowly over time, like a fine wine that improves with age.

The Marriage Trap

You need a partner who will love, cherish and obey you, the emphasis sometimes being on obey. Unfortunately, the Capricorn need for control comes into your relationships as well. As you are terrified of humiliation and loss of dignity, you may only feel confident when you're in charge and calling the shots. You tend to like to know where your partner is all the time. Capricorns can be uncontrollably jealous – but it won't show on the surface. Instead, you just become remote and frosty. When secure in a relationship, you are free to lighten up and your wonderful organising skills can help build a solid and richly satisfying partnership and family dynasty.

Earthy Capricorn

It may take a while to warm you up, but not for nothing do goats get the reputation for lust. Being an earth sign, you know how to enjoy the sensual pleasures of the body and bedchamber. Just don't let your attention to duty get in the way of giving yourself plenty of time off to savour them – even if it means putting an entry in your appointment diary to remind yourself that today's the day you owe it to yourself to have that well-deserved roll in the hay.

SIX

Aspects of the Sun

PLANETS, JUST LIKE PEOPLE, CAN HAVE IMPORTANT RELATIONSHIPS WITH EACH other. These relationships are called aspects. Aspects to your Sun from any other planet can influence your personality markedly. The most powerful effects come with those from the slower-moving planets – Saturn, Uranus, Neptune or Pluto. Sometimes they can alter your ideas about yourself and your behaviour patterns so much that you may not feel at all typical of your sign in certain areas of your life.

Check if your birth date and year appear in the various sections below to find out if one or more of these planets was aspecting the Sun when you were born. Only the so-called challenging aspects have been included. These are formed when the planets are together, opposite or at right angles to each other in the sky.

Unfortunately, because space is restricted, other aspects have been left out, although they have similar effects to those described below and, for the same reason, a few dates will inevitably have been missed out, too. (You can find out for sure whether or not your Sun is aspected at my website www.janeridderpatrick.com) If your Sun has no aspects to Saturn, Uranus, Neptune or Pluto you're more likely to be a typical Capricorn.

Some well-known Capricorns with challenging aspects to their Suns appear below. You can find more in the birthday section at the end of the book.

Sun in Capricorn in Aspect with Saturn

If you were born between 1929–32, 1959–62 or 1988–90, whether or not your birthday is listed below, you are likely to feel the influence of Saturn on your Sun.

21–31 December in: 1930, 1938–9, 1944–5, 1950–51, 1959–60, 1967–8, 1973–4, 1980–81, 1988–9 and 1996–7

1–10 January in: 1930–31, 1938–9, 1951–2, 1959–61, 1968–9, 1974–5, 1980–82, 1989–90 and 1997–8

11–20 January in: 1931–2, 1939–40, 1945–6, 1952–3, 1960–62, 1968–9, 1976, 1982–3, 1990–91 and 1998–9

Quentin Crisp	Nigella Lawson	Henry Miller
Dolly Parton	Harold Shipman	Diane Keaton

This isn't the easiest of aspects. Even by Capricorn standards, it can bring more than its fair share of hardship and responsibility, usually in the first half of life. The cloud does, however, have a substantial silver lining. Saturn is a hard taskmaster, but a fair one. If you play by his rules – patience, hard work, realism and honesty – you will, in the long run, achieve your goals and often much more besides. The secret is not to give in to the periodic depressions that can dog you, or to a sense of futility and despair. Your workaholic tendencies keep you narrowly focused, but don't forget about fun. Author and sex guru Henry Miller said that he didn't start to feel young until he was over forty.

You are driven by a powerful ambition to make

something of your life and to be recognised as one of the elect in your own field. You may feel a little ashamed of this, as you have a secret dread that you are really not good enough and will be found out, judged, found guilty and be punished by being disapproved of or rejected. If you have been harshly treated yourself, especially in childhood, you may be tempted to be judgmental or even hurtful towards others. This may make you feel superior for a while but will leave you miserable and empty inside.

You won't find peace from your nagging self-doubts or a real sense of achievement until you stop looking for outside approval and set your own standards for what success means for you, then work responsibly to create and express your own best self, and make a worthwhile contribution to society at the same time.

Sun in Capricorn in Aspect with Uranus

If you were born between 1988 and 1995, whether or not your birthday is listed below, you are likely to feel the influence of Uranus on your Sun.

21–31 December in: 1930–31, 1948–51, 1968–70 and 1988–91
1–10 January in: 1931–2, 1952–4 and 1991–94
11–20 January in: 1933–6, 1954–6, 1972–5 and 1993–6

Benjamin Franklin	Clara Barton	Simone de Beauvoir
Kevin Costner	Kate Moss	Rudyard Kipling

While you've a great respect for tradition, you are well aware that it is not the be-all and end-all and that progress and change are important, too, if society is to flourish. As social issues concern you, you may have strong political ideals and nonconformist, and sometimes rather controversial, solutions to society's ills. You can see straight to the heart of injustice, inequality and official stupidity, and may be a gifted innovator and inventor. Some people, though, could see you as a bit of an oddball or even downright contrary.

It's not always easy to stand out on a limb, as you may often have to do, but your high principles and Capricorn dedication to being dutiful to what you feel is right will stand you in good stead. You function best when you're working on cutting-edge projects which will then go on to be mainstream – preferably with you as their figurehead. Clara Barton was a nurse who struggled with bureaucracy for years to set up the American Red Cross and became its first president, a position she held for 22 years. It was her tireless campaigning, too, that resulted in the US signing the Geneva Convention, an international agreement to give neutrality to medical workers in war.

Your father may not have been around much, either literally or emotionally, as you were growing up and you may yourself be more comfortable in relationships that are unconventional and allow you plenty of freedom. Simone de Beauvoir, whose book *The Second Sex* was one of the first classics of the modern feminist movement, had a long-term, uncommitted and open relationship with the philosopher Jean-Paul Sartre. Being nailed down rarely appeals to you either, though you can be loyal and steadfast – in your own way.

Sun in Capricorn in Aspect with Neptune
If you were born between 1984 and 1998, whether or not your birthday is listed below, you are likely to feel the influence of Neptune on your Sun.

21–31 December in: 1941–7 and 1983–9
1–10 January in: 1946–51 and 1988–94

11–20 January in: 1951–6 and 1993–9

| Mary Archer | David Bowie | Marlene Dietrich |
| Danny Kaye | Richard Nixon | Albert Schweitzer |

Things are never quite what they seem when Neptune is involved. Instinctively, you tap into people's yearnings and long to fulfil them. This makes you a natural for working in films, advertising, music, the caring professions or – if you're unscrupulous – as a con artist. It's hard to get to know the real you; sometimes even you aren't sure who you are yourself. Others may see you as a saviour or icon or, occasionally, a victim.

Something in you may feel flawed, helpless and dissatisfied, no matter how well your life is going, and you can seesaw between feeling worthless and master or mistress of the universe. With your chronic ache for something just out of reach, your strong escapist tendencies make you long to shift out of everyday reality onto a different plane. It's best if your escapism doesn't involve alcohol or food. Far better options are losing yourself in a good book, music, poetry, art or simply just daydreaming, like Danny Kaye's character Walter Mitty, who created a fantasy life for himself.

This aspect is, at core, a spiritual one and lasting joy comes through finding an ideal to serve and then pouring your whole heart into earthing it. Nobel Peace Prize winner Albert Schweitzer was a medical missionary and musician. At 21, he decided he would live for science and art until he was 30 and then devote his life to serving humanity. This he did. Despite having achieved an international reputation as an organist at such an early age, as well as being principal of a theological college, he gave it all up to study medicine and build a hospital for lepers in Africa. While you might not reach such saintly heights, the sky's the limit for what you can achieve, provided you focus on something that is bigger than your own ego.

Sun in Capricorn in Aspect with Pluto

21–31 December in: 1971–6
1–10 January in: 1930–32 and 1975–80
11–20 January in: 1930–36 and 1979–84

Muhammad Ali	Ava Gardner	Janis Joplin
Martin Luther King	Elvis Presley	J.D. Salinger

Pluto means power and this will come into your life in one form or another. Either you'll be the one wielding the power or at some stage you may, in the form of other people, fate, illness or overwhelming compulsions, find yourself in the grip of a power greater than yourself. Despite success, you could have a sense of being in some way unwanted or unacceptable. This is simply because of your acute sensitivity to emotional undercurrents, especially the slightest whiff of threat or disapproval coming your way.

You can be a force for transforming the world around you, for good or ill. Martin Luther King had the courage to stand up against centuries of ingrained racial prejudice even though it cost him his life. Like him, your libido can be strong. King used sex as a form of anxiety reduction and the FBI tried to blackmail him into suicide by sending tapes to his wife of him having sex with another woman.

This aspect can give you the ability to make a lot of money, or to work with other people's assets. Your will and determination to succeed are formidable, and when you set your mind on some course of action, nobody and nothing is going to be allowed to stand in your way. Be careful, though, not to be too pushy and, inadvertently, put people's backs up. You may be fascinated by taboo subjects and enjoy investigating shady areas, psychological or physical, that other people prefer to avoid. As you don't find it easy to trust, you may be rather secretive and self-protective. You are likely to go through major life stages where you leave your past behind, like world champion boxer Cassius Clay, who transformed himself into Muhammad Ali.

SEVEN

Meeting Your Moon

꡴ THE GLYPH FOR THE MOON IS THE SEMI-CIRCLE OR CRESCENT. It is a symbol for the receptiveness of the soul and is associated with feminine energies and the ebb and flow of the rhythms of life. In some traditions it represents the gateway to paradise and the realms of bliss.

The Sun and Moon are the two complementary poles of your personality, like yang and yin, masculine and feminine, active and reflective, career and home, father and mother. The Moon comes into its own as a guide at night, the time of sleeping consciousness. It also has a powerful effect on the waters of the earth. Likewise, the Moon in your birth chart describes what you respond to instinctively and feel 'in your waters', often just below the level of consciousness. It is your private radar system, sending you messages via your body responses and feelings, telling you whether a situation seems safe or scary, nice or nasty. Feelings provide vital information about circumstances in and around you. Ignore them at your peril; that will lead you into emotional, and sometimes even physical, danger. Eating disorders tend to be associated with being out of touch with, or neglecting, the instincts and the body, both of which the Moon describes.

Extraordinary though it might seem to those who are emotionally tuned in, some people have great difficulty in knowing what they are feeling. One simple way is to pay attention to your body. Notice any sensations that attract your attention. Those are linked to your feelings. Now get a sense of whether they are pleasant or unpleasant, then try to put a more exact name to what those feelings might be. Is it sadness, happiness, fear? What is it that they are trying to tell you? Your Moon hints at what will strongly activate your feelings. Learning to trust and decode this information will help make the world seem – and be – a safer place.

The Moon represents your drive to nurture and protect yourself and others. Its sign, house and aspects describe how you respond and adapt emotionally to situations and what feeds you, in every sense of the word. It gives information about your home and home life and how you experienced your mother, family and childhood, as well as describing your comfort zone of what feels familiar – the words 'family' and 'familiar' come from the same source. It shows, too, what makes you feel secure and what could comfort you when you're feeling anxious. Your Moon describes what moves and motivates you powerfully at the deepest instinctual level and indicates what is truly the 'matter' in – or with – your life.

Knowing children's Moon signs can help parents and teachers better understand their insecurities and respect their emotional make-up and needs, and so prevent unnecessary hurt, or even harm, to sensitive young lives. It's all too easy to expect that our children and parents should have the same emotional wiring as we do, but that's rarely how life works. Finding our parents' Moon signs can be a real revelation. It can often help us understand where they are coming from, what they need and why they react to us in the way they do. Many of my clients have been able to find the understanding and compassion to forgive their parents when they realised that they were doing their very best with the emotional resources available to them.

In relationships it is important that your Moon's requirements are met to a good enough extent. For example, if you have your Moon in Sagittarius you must have adventure, freedom and the opportunity to express your beliefs. If being with your partner constantly violates these basic needs, you will never feel secure and loved and the relationship could, in the long term, undermine you. However, if your Moon feels too comfortable, you will never change and grow. The art is to get a good working balance between support and challenge.

A man's Moon sign can show some of the qualities he will unconsciously select in a wife or partner. Some of the others are shown in his Venus sign. Many women can seem much more like their Moon signs than their Sun signs, especially if they are involved in mothering a family and being a support system for their husbands or partners. It is only at the mid-life crisis that many women start to identify more with the qualities of their own Suns rather than living that out through their partners' ambitions. Similarly, men tend to live out the characteristics of their Moon signs through their wives and partners until mid-life, often quite cut off from their own feelings and emotional responses. If a man doesn't seem at all like his Moon sign, then check out the women in his life. There's a good chance that his wife, mother or daughter will show these qualities.

Your Moon can be in any sign, including the same one as your Sun. Each sign belongs to one of the four elements: Fire, Earth, Air or Water. The element of your Moon can give you a general idea of how you respond to new situations and what you need to feel safe and comforted. We all become anxious if our Moon's needs are not being recognised and attended to. We then, automatically, go into our personal little rituals for making ourselves feel better. Whenever you are feeling distressed, especially when you are way out of your comfort zone in an unfamiliar situation, do something to feed and soothe your Moon. You're almost certain to calm down quickly.

Fire Moons

If you have a Fire Moon in Aries, Leo or Sagittarius, your first response to any situation is to investigate in your imagination the possibilities for drama, excitement and self-expression. Feeling trapped by dreary routine in an ordinary humdrum life crushes you completely. Knowing that you are carrying out a special mission feeds your soul. To you, all the world's a stage and a voyage of discovery. Unless you are at the centre of the action playing some meaningful role, anxiety and depression can set in. To feel secure, you have to have an appropriate outlet for expressing your spontaneity, honourable instincts and passionate need to be of unique significance. The acknowledgement, appreciation and feedback of people around you are essential, or you don't feel real. Not to be seen and appreciated, or to be overlooked, can feel like a threat to your very existence.

Earth Moons

If you have an Earth Moon in Taurus, Virgo or Capricorn, you'll respond to new situations cautiously and practically. Rapidly changing circumstances where you feel swept along and out of control are hard for you to cope with. You need time for impressions to sink in. Sometimes it is only much later, after an event has taken place, that you become sure what you felt about it. Your security lies in slowing down, following familiar routines and rituals, even if they are a bit obsessive, and focusing on something, preferably material – possibly the body itself or nature – which is comforting because it is still there. Indulging the senses in some way often helps too, through food, sex or body care. So does taking charge of the practicalities of the immediate situation, even if this is only mixing the drinks or passing out clipboards. To feel secure, you need continuity and a sense that you have your hand on the rudder of your own life. Think of the rather irreverent joke about the man seeming to cross himself in a crisis, all the while actually touching his most valued possessions to check that they are still intact – spectacles, testicles, wallet and watch. That must have been thought up by someone with the Moon in an earth sign.

Air Moons

When your Moon is in an air sign – Gemini, Libra or Aquarius – you feel most secure when you can stand back from situations and observe them from a distance. Too much intimacy chokes you and you'll tend to escape it by going into your head to the safety of ideas and analysis. Even in close relationships you need your mental, and preferably physical, space. You often have to think, talk or write about what you are feeling before you are sure what your feelings are. By putting them 'out there' so that you can examine them clearly, you can claim them as your own. Unfairness and unethical behaviour can upset you badly and make you feel uneasy until you have done something about it or responded in some way. It can be easy with an air Moon to be unaware of, or to ignore, your own feelings because you are more responsive to ideas, people and situations outside of yourself that may seem to have little connection with you. This is not a good idea, as it cuts you off from the needs of your body as well as your own emotional intelligence. Making opportunities to talk, play with and exchange ideas and information can reduce the stress levels if anxiety strikes.

Water Moons

Finally, if your Moon is in a water sign – Cancer, Scorpio or Pisces – you are ultra-sensitive to atmospheres, and you can experience other people's pain or distress as if they were your own. You tend to take everything personally and, even if the situation has nothing at all to do with you, feel responsible for making it better. Your worst nightmare is to feel no emotional response coming back from other people. That activates your deep-seated terror of abandonment, which can make you feel that you don't exist and is, quite literally, what you fear even more than death. If you feel insecure, you may be tempted to resort to emotional manipulation to try to force intimacy with others – not a good idea, as this can lead to the very rejection that you dread. You are at your most secure when the emotional climate is positive and you have trusted, supportive folk around who will winkle you out of hiding if you become too reclusive. With a water Moon, it is vital to learn to value your own feelings and to take them seriously – and to have a safe, private place you can retreat to when you feel emotionally fragile. As you never forget anything which has made a feeling impression on you, sometimes your reactions are triggered by unconscious memories of things long past, rather than what is taking place in the present. When you learn to interpret them correctly, your feelings are your finest ally and will serve you well.

Finding Your Moon Sign

If you don't yet know your Moon sign, before looking it up, you could have some fun reading through the descriptions that follow and seeing if you can guess which one it is. To find your Moon sign, check your year and date of birth in the tables on pp.98–111. For a greater in-depth understanding of your Moon sign, you might like to read about its characteristics in the book in this series about that sign.

At the beginning of each section are the names of some well-known Capricorns with that particular Moon sign. You can find more about them in Chapter Ten.

Sun in Capricorn with Moon in Aries

Elizabeth Arden	Al Capone	E.M. Forster
William Fox	Heidi Fleiss	Nigella Lawson

If you can find a way of linking your hot, passionate wilfulness with your capacity for hard work, there is very little that will stand in the way of your achieving your heart's desire, whether this is sewing up a city like gangster Al Capone or building a movie empire like William (20th Century) Fox. The tougher the task, the better you like it.

The trouble is, it's not always easy to keep your fiery temper under control so you can find yourself all too frequently in run-ins with others, especially authorities. 'Least said, soonest mended' is a useful motto, but in the heat of the moment your impulsiveness and bossiness can let you down. Dramatic and self-centred, you make an excellent actor, on or off a stage. Boredom and a peaceful, humdrum life would be intolerable to you.

You need to be careful not to be high-handed, as it's not

always easy for you to appreciate another's point of view. You are not exactly subtle and can be rather insensitive about other people's agendas or feelings but your unshakable belief in your own projects can make you an inspiring leader and a force to be reckoned with. You make a brilliant entrepreneur, too, combining shrewd business sense and awesome self-promotional skills. With your strong independent streak, you can't bear being told what to do. You much prefer to be in the driving seat and in total control in every situation, and are fully prepared to battle to hold that position. Your challenge is to learn to stick up for yourself, but without locking horns with authorities or trying to bulldoze your way to success.

Sun in Capricorn with Moon in Taurus

Princess Alexandra   Arthur Scargill   Linda Lovelace
Compton Mackenzie   Madame de   Conrad Hilton
                        Pompadour

The practical and common-sense approach you bring to whatever life throws at you, plus your willingness to take up a position of responsibility, makes you a natural leader. The quiet determination that comes from your core is calming and reassuring. Driven by a desire for security and on-going stability, for yourself and those you serve, you work away quietly to create as safe a nest – and nest-egg – as you possibly can. Not owning your own home would be hard for you. Having a cupboard – or bank balance – as bare as Mother Hubbard's would be almost unthinkable. Contentment for you lies in the simple, sensual pleasures of life – the smell, feel and taste of a lover's skin and your favourite beautiful objects all around. Art and music feed your soul and food will always be of interest. When events change too fast, and you feel swept away out of control, you'll head straight back to the reassurance of these basics. When Princess Alexandra was engaged, her fiancé gave her a dozen sets of silk underwear – a perfect gift for a woman with a Taurus Moon.

You love to be in control and you'll quietly and steadily plod away until you have achieved whatever it is you've set your heart on, doggedly dealing with one obstacle after another as they come along until all resistance is worn down. You are a bit like the irresistible force and the immovable object rolled into one, but beware of slipping into dictator mode when you feel insecure. Stepping off the work treadmill at regular intervals and recharging your batteries at the slow pace of your own heartbeat is essential for your well-being, preferably in the garden or countryside.

Sun in Capricorn with Moon in Gemini

Rowan Atkinson	Joan Baez	Victor Borge
John Delorean	Rudyard Kipling	Liz Lochhead

You are fascinated by just about everything, for a moment or two at least, and being incurably curious, and sometimes downright nosy, you probably enjoy keeping up with all the latest gossip. Like John Delorean, you may be an expert salesman, making what you have to sell seem simply irresistible. He managed to convince governments to part with millions on what later turned out to be less than sure-fire schemes. You can talk yourself into – and out of – just about any situation. The Moon in Gemini has a way with words and you probably never stop using them, and bending them into pretzel shapes. With your sparkling, needle-sharp wit, which often has a dash of vinegar or black comedy added, you've the ability to bring together incongruous ideas with hilarious results.

You are impatient with too much routine and your love of freedom and a hunger for novelty mean you can't bear to be tied down, either physically or mentally. Being constantly on the move is more your style. Putting down roots in one place isn't always easy either; you may even prefer two places you can call your home. Like the child you are at heart, you've a low boredom threshold, but your capacity for wonder should keep you fresh and frisky well into old age. You like to keep up-to-date with what's happening in your field and are often the first to spot a new trend and to capitalise on it. You can be brilliant at lateral thinking and finding solutions to both theoretical and practical problems. Being able to communicate is as essential to you as breathing and keeping a journal or having people around with whom you can share your experiences is almost essential for your sanity. Sometimes it's only by writing or talking about them that you find out what your feelings really are.

Sun in Capricorn with Moon in Cancer

Anthony Clare	Janis Joplin	Telly Savalas
Carol Smillie	Doris Stokes	John Thaw

Do you remember the old TV series *Kojak* where Telly Savalas played the bald cop who was forever sucking lollipops and saying 'Who loves ya, baby'? You may not be so upfront and obvious about it, but, behind your strong and adult 'I can cope with anything' exterior, you too have a little child who wants to be indulged and comforted. Men with this combination can make women want to mother them, as the mix of tough yet tender and reserved yet vulnerable is often irresistible – like John Thaw's most popular character, Inspector Morse.

Without the safety net of emotional, financial and domestic security to fall back on, you can become quite ungrounded. Home and family matter a great deal to you and you can make a wonderful parent or mentor. Your imagination and inner life can be creative but you may be afraid to show it, as you're terrified of being excluded or humiliated. This could make you act cynical in self-protection. Or you could try to crash through other people's boundaries to be accepted and experience the rejection you fear. Being rather touchy, it is all too easy for you to take criticism, real or imagined, far too personally and withdraw into sulking, blame and grumpiness. Your ability to tune in to the feelings of those around makes it easy for you to establish a rapport with almost everyone. Anthony Clare interviews celebrities in his radio programme, *In the Psychiatrist's Chair*. With his gentleness and compassionate understanding, he has a knack of getting people to share even their most private experiences on air. You too have the ability to make others feel cherished and safe. Learning to deal with your rollercoaster emotions and using your emotional intelligence skilfully will pay rich dividends in every area of your life.

Sun in Capricorn with Moon in Leo

Marlene Dietrich	Robert Bly	David Bowie
St Bernadette of Lourdes	Faye Dunaway	Mao Tse-tung

Your Leo Moon needs a role to play and plenty of admiring attention to keep you feeling secure, so you'll tend to dress beautifully. Success, status and a prominent place in the limelight are what feed you and your challenge is to make sure that the role you take on brings out the best – responsible leadership – and not the worst – self-centred dictatorship – that you are capable of. A career that demands performing, in any way, is right up your street. One courageous person I know with this combination, despite serious health problems that required repeated surgery, entertained doctors royally right up to the time the anaesthetic kicked in, and became known as their star patient.

Being overlooked or feeling insignificant can make you anxious. You hate to have your dignity ruffled or to be seen in a bad light. You've a knack of getting your way, and with your natural charisma and commanding presence, any opposition to your plans usually quickly melts away. If you feel overlooked or aren't shown the proper respect you believe is your right, you can sometimes become touchy, haughty and frostily disapproving. You may have to watch a tendency to be patronising and to take yourself too seriously. Overlooking the fact that the plans and preferences of other people are important too can lead to trouble.

Playing with children can help bring out the spontaneous child in you, and allow you to drop, for a while at least, your workaholic tendencies. Sometimes a Leo Moon indicates that you come from a prominent family or that you have a powerful, dramatic or even domineering mother. It certainly means that you are at your best in a home you can be proud of.

Sun in Capricorn with Moon in Virgo

| Tycho Brahe | Oliver Hardy | Aristotle Onassis |
| Dolly Parton | Susan Sontag | Samuel Smiles |

You can have a matter-of-fact and practical attitude to doing whatever needs to be done to achieve your goals, even if this involves tackling tasks that other people would find boring or insignificant. In any creative fields you make a skilled artist and craftsperson, going to endless trouble to get the finished article just right. Dolly Parton, queen of chest enhancement and tackiness, once said that she isn't offended by dumb blonde jokes because she knows she isn't dumb, and then added – 'I also know I'm not blonde.' Chuckling all the way to the bank, she confides 'It takes a lot of money to make a person look this cheap.' Whatever you do, whether it's over-the-top or understated, you'll pay close attention to detail.

You may need to guard against a tendency to be fiercely critical, both of yourself and others, when things don't come up to your sometimes impossibly high standards. While you'll enjoy ticking off achievements on those never-ending to-do lists that whirr round in your head, it's best not to let them run your life. You no doubt share with Samuel Smiles, author of the Victorian bestseller *Self Help*, a belief in the 'gospel of work'. He added to the proverb 'All work and no play makes Jack a dull boy' the line 'But all play and no work makes him something worse'. You may have an interest in body care or be drawn to the healing professions, where you could excel. When you feel insecure, you may push yourself to work even harder and end up frazzled. Your nervous system is highly-strung so quiet time alone for rest, recuperation and reflection is essential. Simplicity suits you, so cutting down to essentials, dejunking your life and detoxing your body could be a perfect tonic from time to time.

Sun in Capricorn with Moon in Libra

Nicolas Cage	Dyan Cannon	Joe Frazier
William Gladstone	Del Shannon	Susannah York

Your strong sense of justice means that you are likely to be a fair and even-handed boss. Some with this combination are drawn to politics. William Gladstone, despite his reputation of being a crusty Victorian prime minister, was well ahead of his time in attempting to rescue and rehabilitate prostitutes. (Though his motives, said some, were not entirely pure and high-minded.) Being a first-class diplomat, you can smoothly and competently find backing and support for whatever scheme you have set your mind on – to the extent that others almost think it was their idea in the first place. If you feel that you have offended someone, or sense disharmony and discontent around you, you'll be ill at ease until peace and unity have been restored. In your passion for fairness, you can be too altruistic and overlook what is fair for you, then the pendulum will swing back and you may brood on how badly you've been treated.

Even if you are not conventionally beautiful, there is likely to be something about you that others find attractive and elegant. Most people with Libra Moons prefer to be well turned-out and take pains to look their best in most situations. Manners matter to you and coarseness and lack of respect for others can put your back up. Men with this combination tend to have well-developed caring, empathetic feminine sides and can even be rather dandyish without any compromise whatsoever to their masculinity. They are also often well-disposed to doing their fair share of housework and childcare. If you are a woman, you can combine all of the feminine graces with the strength of will and mind traditionally associated with men and can be formidable, while gracious, in business.

Sun in Capricorn with Moon in Scorpio

Shirley Bassey	Ralph Fiennes	Hermann Goering
Nostradamus	Cynthia Payne	Rod Stewart

Sex, death, secrets, survival and evil are recurrent themes in your life. Even if your childhood was happy, you would have been acutely aware of forbidden topics and of powerfully charged emotional atmospheres and may have witnessed the use or misuse of power. Home, or belonging to your particular family, may not always have felt a safe place to be. Like sultry Ralph Fiennes, you could exude an aura of sexual charisma, all the more enticing as it is usually reined in tightly, and may be able to capitalise on this in your career. Your feel for power and money, combined with your determination and capacity for hard work, can lead to wealth if you so choose, especially if you refuse to feel intimidated and crushed by those in control.

    You are constantly vigilant to threats to your security and that of your home and family, and will take steps to protect them. With a Scorpio Moon, you feel intensely and this can move you, occasionally, to over-react by withdrawing or destroying. Hermann Goering, who founded the Gestapo and set up the concentration camps, tipped this intensity into paranoia and brought about the deaths of millions. We can see some of the Scorpio preoccupation with threat and death too in the dire predictions of Nostradamus, who seemed to have a nose for doom and disaster. To keep buoyant, you may need to empty your emotional septic tanks frequently, as your tendency to cling on to fear and resentment can make you bitter. Fortunately, most with this combination are passionately preoccupied with ensuring that the vulnerable are protected and the best traditions in society are upheld whilst those that are outworn or oppressive are discarded. You have the potential for great sensuality and powerful leadership. The art is to employ and enjoy these responsibly.

Sun in Capricorn with Moon in Sagittarius

| Cecil Beaton | Kevin Costner | Umberto Eco |
| Anthony Hopkins | Alexander Woollcott | Madam C.J. Walker |

The writer Alexander Woollcott noted forlornly that all the things he liked to do were illegal, immoral or fattening. Your Capricorn Sun is chained to duty and the tradition of hard work while your Sagittarius Moon wants to skip off and have fun and not even consider laws, morality or calorie content. Your challenge is to find a time and place in your life to prise the stern adult disciplinarian off your back so that you can enjoy the sensation of the wind in your hair and the exultation of unrestrained high spirits.

You need to be able to move about freely and investigate the world around you. At 18, Kevin Costner built his own canoe and paddled down rivers that early explorers had navigated to the Pacific. Your adventurous spirit may lead you into the world of ideas and knowledge. Whatever you choose, you like to paint on a large canvas; Umberto Eco, author of the bestselling *The Name of the Rose*, speaks five languages fluently and has over a dozen honorary doctorates. Something about his exuberance and wide span of learning could appeal to you. Enterprise is in your blood. You are able to see possibilities in every situation, and may even be a bit of an opportunist. You can, however, also be breathtakingly generous with your time and resources. Madam C. J. Walker, the first African-American woman millionaire, made her fortune with her hair-straightening treatment and a substantial social contribution in her work to end lynching and to obtain women's rights. You have so much potential for enjoying life to the full, so it's important that you don't allow duty to take over and rule your life.

Sun in Capricorn with Moon in Capricorn

| Clara Barton | Richard Briers | William James |
| Annie Lennox | Warren Mitchell | Tracey Ullman |

With your tight self-discipline and ability to plan long-term, you're a hard act to beat. Once you've set your sights on a goal, you will stick at it doggedly, overcoming every obstacle until success is yours. The problem is that you have a discouraging inner judge that can make your life miserable if you let it have its way. Hard work and shouldering heavy responsibilities are as familiar to you as breathing. Many with this combination have come from humble backgrounds and work their way steadily to the top, or were raised in homes where correct behaviour and discipline were the rule, rather than spontaneity and warm acceptance. There's a bonus in this – you are well able to look after yourself, and unless you give in to hopelessness or depression, you can build a great life for yourself. You make a loyal and responsible partner but it is important to resist the temptation to put your home life in second place to your work and ambitions.

The nagging fear of failure and rejection by the powers that be can keep you chronically insecure until you become part of the establishment yourself. It's important not to keep looking back to some mythical golden age of the past where everything was much better than the way things are today; that's a sure-fire recipe for turning sour and bigoted like Alf Garnett, the character that Warren Mitchell plays in *Till Death Us Do Part*. As you sense that solitude and sinking into melancholy feed you, you may defend your privacy fiercely. It's important to allow yourself plenty of time alone and remember to stop from time to time to recognise, and enjoy, your hard-earned achievements.

Sun in Capricorn with Moon in Aquarius

Muhammad Ali	Joseph Smith	Diane Keaton
Richard Nixon	Bonnie Prince Charlie	Denzel Washington

It's not always easy for you to know what your feelings are, as you respond more readily to the needs of society at large than your own. While having a strong sense of community, you could have trouble fitting into a close-knit and exclusive conventional family unit. You can be a brilliant strategist and your mission is to improve the way the world operates, whatever the cost to yourself.

Your moods can be quite contrary. One moment you'll be cool and withdrawn, then you'll turn chatty and friendly the next. You may even neglect to feed, water and exercise your body unless you are prompted. Others may see you as aloof and abrupt, and possibly even a bit of an oddball or loner – often ahead of the crowd in your ideas and passions. Diane Keaton started a fashion trend with her unisex clothes and her awkward, gawky mannerisms.

You like things logical and clear-cut. Messy emotions can disturb you, your own just as much as other people's. You are much more at ease with loyal friendships than intimacy and if anybody tries to get too close, either physically or emotionally, you'll start to feel jittery and trapped. Your home is likely to be unusual or unconventional in some way, and even if you have lived in the same house all your life, you may feel as though you are just camping temporarily, slightly on edge, waiting for the call to move on. This can stop you putting down emotional roots anywhere so you need a partner who will give you the space you need, and allow your home to be open house to fresh people and ideas.

Sun in Capricorn with Moon in Pisces

Joan of Arc	Marianne Faithfull	Martin Luther King
Tara Palmer-Tomkinson	Elvis Presley	Dennis Wheatley

Being so emotionally sensitive, you need to choose carefully whom you allow into your intimate space. It's all too easy for you to be sucked into other people's realities and be pushed around, seduced or manipulated by stronger personalities. The positive side of this is that you are equally open to the power of beauty and goodness and love, and may be a natural healer. You empathise instinctively with other people's pain and can walk into a room and pick up atmospheres, noticing especially if someone is suffering or expecting something from you. You'll then feel uncomfortable until you have supplied whatever you sense they need. As a child, you probably felt responsible for looking after your mother and learned to read emotional atmospheres in order to have your own needs met indirectly.

You've the gift of tapping in to other people's longings and giving them expression. The civil-rights activist Martin Luther King, who advocated non-violence, was an inspiration for millions with his moving 'I have a dream . . .' speech. You, too, need a dream, as your finest qualities develop when you find an ideal to serve and then give your all to realising it.

Because of your susceptibility to free-floating anxieties, and to feeling haunted by a sense of flawedness, it's important to avoid retreating from the world into fantasy, fear, dependency or even addiction. Elvis Presley, despite having everything material that could be wished for, spent his last years obese, drug-dependent and under the control of his domineering manager. A Pisces Moon more often than not means mess at home, literally or metaphorically, but it is best to view this as creative chaos, useful for stimulating your imagination for higher things.

EIGHT

Mercury – It's All in the Mind

☿ THE GLYPHS FOR THE PLANETS ARE MADE UP OF THREE SYMBOLS: the circle, the semi-circle and the cross. Mercury is the only planet, apart from Pluto, whose glyph is made up of all three of these symbols. At the bottom there is the cross, representing the material world; at the top is the semi-circle of the crescent Moon, symbolising the personal soul; and in the middle, linking these two, is the circle of eternity, expressed through the individual. In mythology, Mercury was the only god who had access to all three worlds – the underworld, the middle world of earth and the higher world of the gods. Mercury in your chart represents your ability, through your thoughts and words, to make connections between the inner world of your mind and emotions, the outer world of other people and events, and the higher world of intuition. Your Mercury sign can give you a great deal of information about the way your mind works and about your interests, communication skills and your preferred learning style.

It can be frustrating when we just can't get through to some people and it's easy to dismiss them as being either completely thick or deliberately obstructive. Chances are they are neither. It may be that you're simply not talking each other's languages. Knowing your own and other people's communication styles can lead to major breakthroughs in relationships.

Information about children's natural learning patterns can help us teach them more effectively. It's impossible to learn properly if the material isn't presented in a way that resonates with the way your mind works. You just can't 'hear' it, pick it up or grasp it. Wires then get crossed and the data simply isn't processed. Many children are seriously disadvantaged if learning materials and environments don't speak to them. You may even have been a child like that yourself. If so, you could easily have been left with the false impression that you are a poor learner just because you couldn't get a handle on the lessons being taught. Identifying your own learning style can be like finding the hidden key to the treasure room of knowledge.

The signs of the zodiac are divided into four groups by element:

> The fire signs: Aries, Leo and Sagittarius
> The earth signs: Taurus, Virgo and Capricorn
> The air signs: Gemini, Libra and Aquarius
> The water signs: Cancer, Scorpio and Pisces

Your Mercury will therefore belong to one of the four elements, depending on which sign it is in. Your Mercury can only be in one of three signs – the same sign as your Sun, the one before or the one after. This means that each sign has one learning style that is never natural to it. For Capricorn, this is the water style.

Mercury in each of the elements has a distinctive way of

operating. I've given the following names to the learning and communicating styles of Mercury through the elements. Mercury in fire – active imaginative; Mercury in earth – practical; Mercury in air – logical; and Mercury in water – impressionable.

Mercury in Fire: Active Imaginative

Your mind is wide open to the excitement of fresh ideas. It responds to action and to the creative possibilities of new situations. Drama, games and storytelling are excellent ways for you to learn. You love to have fun and play with ideas. Any material to be learned has to have some significance for you personally, or add to your self-esteem, otherwise you rapidly lose interest. You learn by acting out the new information, either physically or in your imagination. The most efficient way of succeeding in any goal is to make first a mental picture of your having achieved it. This is called mental rehearsal and is used by many top sportsmen and women as a technique to help improve their performance. You do this spontaneously, as your imagination is your greatest mental asset. You can run through future scenarios in your mind's eye and see, instantly, where a particular piece of information or situation could lead and spot possibilities that other people couldn't even begin to dream of. You are brilliant at coming up with flashes of inspiration for creative breakthroughs and crisis management.

Mercury in Earth: Practical

Endless presentations of feelings, theories and possibilities can make your eyes glaze over and your brain ache to shut down. What really turns you on is trying out these theories and possibilities to see if they work in practice. If they don't, you'll tend to classify them 'of no further interest'. Emotionally charged information is at best a puzzling non-starter and at worst an irritating turn-off. Practical demonstrations, tried and tested facts and working models fascinate you. Hands-on learning, where you can see how a process functions from start to finish, especially if it leads to some useful material end-product, is right up your street. It's important to allow yourself plenty of time when you are learning, writing or thinking out what to say, otherwise you can feel rushed and out of control, never pleasant sensations for earth signs. Your special skill is in coming up with effective solutions to practical problems and in formulating long-range plans that bring concrete, measurable results.

Mercury in Air: Logical

You love learning about, and playing with, ideas, theories and principles. Often you do this best by arguing or bouncing ideas off other people, or by writing down your thoughts. Your special gift is in your ability to stand back and work out the patterns of relationship between people or things. You much prefer it when facts are presented to you logically and unemotionally and have very little time for the irrational, uncertainty or for personal opinions. You do, though, tend to have plenty of those kinds of views yourself, only you call them logical conclusions. Whether a fact is useful or not is less important than whether it fits into your mental map of how the world operates. If facts don't fit in, you'll either ignore them, find a way of making them fit, or, occasionally, make a grand leap to a new, upgraded theory. Yours is the mind of the scientist or chess player. You make a brilliant planner because you can be detached enough to take an overview of the entire situation.

Mercury in Water: Impressionable

Your mind is sensitive to atmospheres and emotional undertones and to the context in which information is presented. Plain facts and figures can often leave you cold and even intimidated. You can take things too personally and read between the lines for what you believe is really being said or taught. If you don't feel emotionally safe, you can be cautious about revealing your true thoughts. It may be hard, or even impossible, for you to learn properly in what you sense is a hostile environment. You are excellent at impression management. Like a skilful artist painting a picture, you can influence others to think what you'd like them to by using suggestive gestures or pauses and intonations. People with Mercury in water signs are often seriously disadvantaged by left-brain schooling methods that are too rigidly structured for them. You take in information best through pictures or images, so that you get a 'feel' for the material and can make an emotional bond with it, in the same way you connect with people. In emotionally supportive situations where there is a rapport between you and your instructors, or your learning material, you are able just to drink in and absorb circulating knowledge without conscious effort, sometimes not even being clear about how or why you know certain things.

Finding Your Mercury Sign

If you don't yet know your Mercury sign, you might like to see if you can guess what it is from the descriptions below before checking it out in the tables on pp.112–14.

Sun in Capricorn with Mercury in Sagittarius

Diane Keaton	Sir James Frazer	Rudyard Kipling
St Ignatius Loyola	Doris Stokes	Janet Street-Porter

Thinking small is not your style. Because of your optimism and faith that everything will all work out somehow, you can take on massive projects and sometimes promise in the heat of the moment more than you can comfortably deliver. Always quick to spot an opportunity, you could sell snow to Siberia – and probably manage to negotiate an exclusive government contract while you're about it.

Your vision is broad and your mind wide open to learning from people of every race, creed and culture and making, through this, a significant contribution to understanding others. Sir James Frazer researched the history of world myth and religion and wrote 12 massive volumes entitled *The Golden Bough*, which are classics in their field. For the medium Doris Stokes, death and distance were no object. She appeared to have the ability to speak to the departed and brought great comfort to many mourners.

You are potentially a rousing and inspiring speaker or teacher, as you are fired up with zeal for your subject. There is more than a little of the crusader about you. Saint Ignatius Loyola, who founded the Jesuits, sent out missionaries to Japan, India and Brazil. That was in the 1550s. Just think what you can do with today's facilities!

Your tendency to be outspoken and somewhat tactless could land you in hot water, but your generosity of mind and spirit, and talent for motivating and encouraging others should more than make up for that. Even if you have little formal education, with your thirst for knowledge you are likely to keep yourself well-informed. You learn best when you allow your imagination full rein and learn to distinguish genuine hunches from wild speculation.

Sun in Capricorn with Mercury in Capricorn

| Marlene Dietrich | Nigella Lawson | Richard Nixon |
| Aristotle Onassis | Warren Mitchell | Louis Braille |

You've the mind of a corporate lawyer and can quickly suss out pitfalls in any project you're involved in. You like to feel in control, especially in business deals and contracts, and are inclined to read the small print carefully, searching for snags and loopholes you could use to your advantage. You may have a dismal cast of mind, tut-tutting over the way the world is going to the dogs compared to how it was or should be. If, however, you can avoid being dragged down into gloom and despondency, you can use your realism to move steadily towards substantial long-term goals, seeing setbacks as comforting signposts on the way. At the back of your mind there's usually a master plan for climbing up whatever ladder of success you have chosen for yourself.

Having a practical mind, you probably welcome a formal or traditional approach to learning and may even enjoy taking responsibility for helping others learn. Louis Braille, a blind schoolboy of 12, invented a language of dots which allows visually impaired people to read. Despite disapproval, discouragement and rejections from officialdom, he never gave up even though his system wasn't accepted until after his death.

Some people may find you a little formal or reserved, and even slightly frosty, in the way you communicate and you've probably been told that you have an old head on your shoulders. You like to ponder well before saying anything important. You may sometimes feel that it takes you longer than others to learn and can experience long stretches where spontaneous communication seems blocked, but once you get started it's as if an ice cap has melted and your words flow freely and fluently.

Sun in Capricorn with Mercury in Aquarius

Kevin Costner	Benjamin Franklin	Janis Joplin
Martin Luther King	Linda Lovelace	Dennis Wheatley

Your mind can act as a lightning conductor for ideas that will erupt into world consciousness in the foreseeable future, but are, at the moment, far ahead of their time. While most people are content to go along with the common consensus view of reality, truth – as you see it – matters almost more than anything to you, and you'll speak up and out, whatever the cost to yourself, even if others think you are eccentric or crazy. Your views are frequently unorthodox and, like Janis Joplin did, you may even enjoy raising a few eyebrows or ruffling a feather or two.

Once a notion has lodged in your mind, it can stay there firmly despite all evidence to the contrary. This can give you great tenacity to follow through on your ideas, but can occasionally lead to knuckle-headed stubbornness. You are able to take the long, cool and detached view of anything you come across, viewing facts with interest but very little emotional bias. Patterns fascinate you and you can see how each small piece of information connects with, and affects, life as a whole. Often your insights come with an 'Aha!' like the light bulbs that go on in cartoon characters' minds. You may pick up progressive new ideas that are just starting to circulate and become their mouthpiece. This is an excellent position for a scientist or social reformer. Benjamin Franklin was both. He discovered that lightning and electricity are identical and was an important contributor to the debates that led to the American Declaration of Independence. Sharing your ideas with like-minded people is your idea of mental bliss. Even better is putting your insights to some profitable or humanitarian use which contributes in some way to changing society with long-lasting benefit to all.

NINE

Venus — At Your Pleasure

♀ THE GLYPH FOR VENUS IS MADE UP OF THE CIRCLE OF ETERNITY on top of the cross of matter. Esoterically this represents love, which is a quality of the divine, revealed on earth through personal choice. The saying 'One man's meat is another man's poison' couldn't be more relevant when it comes to what we love. It is a mystery why we find one thing attractive and another unattractive, or even repulsive. Looking at the sign, aspects and house of your Venus can't give any explanation of this mystery, but it can give some clear indications of what it is that you value and find desirable. This can be quite different from what current fashion tells you you should like. For example, many people are strongly turned on by voluptuous bodies but the media constantly shows images of near-anorexics as the desirable ideal. If you ignore what you, personally, find beautiful and try to be, or to love, what at heart leaves you cold, you are setting yourself up for unnecessary pain and dissatisfaction. Being true to your Venus sign, even if other people think you are strange, brings joy and pleasure. It also builds up your self-esteem because it grounds you solidly in your own personal values. This, in turn, makes you much more attractive to others. Not only that, it improves your relationships immeasurably, because you are living authentically and not betraying yourself by trying to prove your worth to others by being something you are not.

Glittering Venus, the brightest planet in the heavens, was named after the goddess of love, war and victory. Earlier names for her were Aphrodite, Innana and Ishtar. She was beautiful, self-willed and self-indulgent but was also skilled in all the arts of civilisation.

Your Venus sign shows what you desire and would like to possess, not only in relationships but also in all aspects of your taste, from clothes and culture to hobbies and hobby-horses. It identifies how and where you can be charming and seductive and skilful at creating your own type of beauty yourself. It also describes your style of attracting partners and the kind of people that turn you on. When your Venus is activated you feel powerful, desirable and wonderfully, wickedly indulged and indulgent. When it is not, even if someone has all the right credentials to make a good match, the relationship will always lack that certain something. If you don't take the chance to express your Venus to a good enough degree somewhere in your life, you miss out woefully on delight and happiness.

Morning Star, Evening Star

Venus appears in the sky either in the morning or in the evening. The ancients launched their attacks when Venus became a morning star, believing that she was then in her warrior-goddess role, releasing aggressive energy for victory in battle. If you're a morning-star person, you're likely to be impulsive, self-willed and idealistic, prepared to hold out until you find the partner who is just right for you.

Relationships and business dealings of morning-star Venus people are said to prosper best whenever Venus in the sky is a morning star. If you are an early bird, you can check this out. At these times Venus can be seen in the eastern sky before the Sun has risen.

The name for Venus as an evening star is Hesperus and it was then, traditionally, said to be sacred to lovers. Evening-star people tend to be easy-going and are open to negotiation, conciliation and making peace. If you are an evening-star Venus person, your best times in relationship and business affairs are said to be when Venus can be seen, jewel-like, in the western sky after the Sun has set.

Because the orbit of Venus is so close to the Sun, your Venus can only be in one of five signs. You have a morning-star Venus if your Venus is in one of the two signs that come before your Sun sign in the zodiac. You have an evening-star Venus if your Venus is in either of the two signs that follow your Sun sign. If you have Venus in the same sign as your Sun, you could be either, depending on whether your Venus is ahead of or behind your Sun. (You can find out which at the author's website www.janeridderpatrick.com.)

If you don't yet know your Venus sign you might like to read through all of the following descriptions and see if you can guess what it is. You can find out for sure on pp.115–18.

At the beginning of each section are the names of some well-known Capricorns with that particular Venus sign. You can find out more about them in Chapter Ten, Famous Capricorn Birthdays.

Sun in Capricorn with Venus in Scorpio

Ralph Fiennes   Ava Gardner   Janet Street-Porter
Denzel Washington   Annie Lennox   Marianne Faithfull

Beneath that restrained and cool exterior, passion simmers. You are intensely private and may be secretive about what is really going on in your life and there can be much agony and ecstasy behind closed doors. You have no time for superficiality and love to push yourself to the limits in both ambition and love. Power and wealth can turn you on and you'll either attract these to yourself or find a partner who does – or both. Your partner may be influential, either personally or in position, and may be intense and rather uncompromising. Occasionally, this placement can indicate abusive or degrading relationships, and if this is your experience know that you have immense power to transform your relationships, especially the one with yourself. Bullies – and that includes your own fears – are cowards. By standing up to them, your strength and self-esteem will grow. Love triangles are another Venus in Scorpio speciality, as extremes excite you and it can be hard to give up the adrenalin rush that comes with cliff-hanging situations.

Part of this pattern comes from the fact that you're looking for total emotional security and are prone to testing your partner to see if he, or she, really does love you. Once you are sure your mate is trustworthy, you are capable of intense and abiding loyalty. With your subtle and sultry sexuality, people can be magnetically drawn to you without being sure exactly why. Mysteries fascinate you and you are drawn to investigate, and do something about it if corruption is involved. Sex is important and if that doesn't work, the relationship could quickly sour. To be fulfilled, you need passion – either in love or in your love of work.

Sun in Capricorn with Venus in Sagittarius

Kahlil Gibran	Rudyard Kipling	Nigella Lawson
Cynthia Payne	Albert Schweitzer	Carol Smillie

You may chose partners who are foreigners or are connected with publishing or broadcasting, travel, the law or religion, or may find joy in these fields yourself. Relationships where you learn from or teach others can bring you immense pleasure, especially if it helps encourage others to bring out the best in themselves or improve their lives in some way. Kahlil Gibran, author of the bestseller *The Prophet*, has inspired thousands with his depth of love and wisdom. No matter how dark life becomes, if you choose, you can summon up reserves of hope and faith in a brighter future and find exactly the right words to uplift those around you, too. Rudyard Kipling's enduringly popular stiffener of the moral fibre, 'If', did just that. In a recent BBC opinion poll, it was voted, overwhelmingly, the nation's favourite poem.

Capricorn is not naturally inclined to frivolity but this placement of Venus can give you a theatrical streak of sheer unabashed mischief – and cheeky free enterprise. Cynthia Payne, who was considered by some MPs, vicars and lawyers to be the hostess with the best meal deal in London, ran a brothel where fun and frolics were exchanged for luncheon vouchers. Foreign places could be an important and much loved part of your life. Albert Schweitzer was drawn to Africa to fulfil his life's work, giving hope to lepers, and an example of philanthropy to the rest of the world.

Whatever your gospel – and you're almost certain to

have one – you'll take enormous pleasure in preaching it with zeal and conviction. You have opinions and no way are you going to keep them to yourself. It would be hard for you to stay committed to a partner who does not either share your beliefs or, alternatively, allow you plenty of freedom to be the free spirit you are.

Sun in Capricorn with Venus in Capricorn

Elizabeth Arden	Benjamin Franklin	A.A. Milne
Aristotle Onassis	Dolly Parton	Elvis Presley

You or your partner can be phenomenally hard-working and enjoy climbing the corporate or social ladder. Elizabeth Arden had little education but built up an international empire of exclusive salons, and, at the beginning of the last century, made cosmetics acceptable to 'respectable' American women. Rarely the most romantic creature, you are rather formal and treat both commitment and fun seriously – and sometimes cynically. Benjamin Franklin advised a lusty young friend to marry, but if he must have affairs, to choose older women, as they are more experienced, discreet, wise – and grateful, adding that, anyway, in the dark all cats are grey. Like him, your realism and ambition rarely desert you even in intimate matters. You believe that a contract, marriage or otherwise, is a contract and needs to cover every eventuality. After divorcing her first husband – whom she had never allowed to own stock in her company – Elizabeth Arden married a foreign prince. You may be drawn to partners who are much younger or older, or who are of a different station in life to you. Aristotle Onassis came from a background far removed from that of Jacqueline Kennedy but their marriage seemed to have been a shrewd deal for both of them.

Your work is so tied up with your pleasure that there's often no clear boundary between the one and the other. You see no reason to waste time and may use holidays to create more business opportunities, or profit. Your pleasures could be simple and solitary – A.A. Milne spent most evenings quietly smoking his pipe and doing a crossword – or, if you have the wherewithal, you may prefer the kinds of vacation, like exclusive cruises to smart destinations, which discreetly signal 'I've made it'.

Sun in Capricorn with Venus in Aquarius

John Thaw	Joseph Smith	Janis Joplin
Marlene Dietrich	Simone de Beauvoir	J.R.R. Tolkien

Warm companionship is often more to your liking than sticky, dark passion. Powerful emotions, especially of the deep and dangerous kind, and too much intimacy, can make you gasp for air. Your natural reserve when it comes to relating can sometimes be mistaken for aloofness – think of the ice-maiden image of Marlene Dietrich – but you are far from cold. You just don't like to be crowded or confined. Friends mean a great deal to you. You can go to extraordinary lengths to help if they are ever in trouble. Being part of a group that's on your wavelength, preferably fighting for some cause that benefits the world, can bring you happiness and a sense of belonging. For a long-lasting commitment, a like-minded partner who shares your ideas and ideals is a must. Sometimes your ideas are nonconformist, to say the least, and you can even take delight in shocking just for the sheer hell of it. Janis Joplin had a wildly rebellious and unconventional lifestyle and was one of the first women to break into the boys' world of rock and roll.

Some Capricorns with Venus in Aquarius are emotionally detached when it comes to sex, notching up conquests on the bedposts, their hearts untouched. Others, once committed, are so highly principled that they would almost rather die than deceive. There could be something quite unconventional in your relationships. Your partner may be much older or younger than you – John Thaw's wife, Sheila Hancock, was 10 years older than him – or from a different social or cultural background. Joseph Smith, who founded the Mormons, introduced the idea of multiple 'spiritual wives' and polygamy. You might not go that far but you do like to run your relationships in your own special way.

Sun in Capricorn with Venus in Pisces

Shirley Bassey	Max Bruch	Molière
Edgar Allan Poe	Rod Stewart	Sophie Tucker

No matter how hard-headed you are in other departments of your life, you have an ideal of perfect bliss that could come through fantasy, beauty or love. Max Bruch's exquisite violin concertos reach towards that musically. You're searching for your prince or princess who will make your dreams come true, save you from suffering, magic away all your inadequacies and protect you from any contact with harsh reality.

You may attract people who are emotionally unavailable, except in your imagination, or who are tinged with tragedy as your strong poetic streak revels in sorrow and unrequited love. Edgar Allan Poe cherished the romantic memory all his life of the mother of a school-friend who had been affectionate towards him, but who went mad and died.

Alternatively, you could attract people who long to be rescued by your strong, and possibly glamorous, presence and want to surrender their will to yours. You may need to check a tendency for confusing pity and sympathy with love or be led astray by a hard-luck story or an alluring, seductive line.

You are capable of devoted, sometimes self-sacrificial and deeply spiritual love. Though yearning for emotional intimacy and the fusion of twinned souls, you may find this hard to express because of your Capricorn discomfort with open displays of emotion. At your best, you'll find profound satisfaction in serving others unselfishly. Sometimes you set your sights so high, looking for the perfect relationship, that you never do take the plunge and commit to one person, as you become deeply disappointed when you discover that potential partners have ordinary human flaws. The secret is to bring in your Capricorn realism and don't expect to find heaven on tap, but revel in it when it appears.

TEN

Famous Capricorn Birthdays

FIND OUT WHO SHARES YOUR MOON, MERCURY AND VENUS SIGNS, and any challenging Sun aspects, and see what they have done with the material they were born with. Notice how often it is not just the personalities of the people themselves but the roles of actors, characters of authors and works of artists that reflect their astrological make-up. In reading standard biographies, I've been constantly astounded – and, of course, delighted – at how often phrases used to describe individuals could have been lifted straight from their astrological profiles. Check it out yourself!

A few people below have been given a choice of two Moons. This is because the Moon changed sign on the day that they were born and no birth time was available. You may be able to guess which one is correct if you read the descriptions of the Moon signs in Chapter Seven.

22 December
1962 Ralph Fiennes, actor, *The English Patient*, *Schindler's List*
Sun aspects: none
Moon: Scorpio   Mercury: Capricorn   Venus: Scorpio

23 December
1805 Joseph Smith, founder of the Mormon Church
Sun aspects: none
Moon: Aquarius   Mercury: Capricorn   Venus: Aquarius

24 December
1922 Ava Gardner, one of the most beautiful actresses ever
Sun aspects: Pluto
Moon: Pisces   Mercury: Capricorn   Venus: Scorpio

25 December
1642 Isaac Newton, physicist, demonstrator of the Law of Gravity
Sun aspects: none
Moon: Cancer   Mercury: Sagittarius   Venus: Aquarius

26 December
1893 Mao Tse-tung, Chinese communist leader, author of the *Little Red Book*
Sun aspects: none
Moon: Leo   Mercury: Sagittarius   Venus: Aquarius

27 December
1901 Marlene Dietrich, sultry German actress, *The Blue Angel*
Sun aspects: Neptune
Moon: Leo   Mercury: Capricorn   Venus: Aquarius

28 December
1954 Denzel Washington, actor, *Cry Freedom*, *Malcolm X*
Sun aspects: none
Moon: Aquarius   Mercury: Capricorn   Venus: Scorpio

29 December
1721 Madame de Pompadour, extravagant mistress of King Louis XV
Sun aspects: none
Moon: Taurus   Mercury: Sagittarius   Venus: Sagittarius

30 December
1865 Rudyard Kipling, author, *The Jungle Book*, *Just So Stories*
Sun aspects: Uranus, Neptune
Moon: Gemini   Mercury: Sagittarius   Venus: Sagittarius

31 December
1878 Elizabeth Arden, founder of cosmetics empire
Sun aspects: none
Moon: Aries   Mercury: Sagittarius   Venus: Capricorn

1 January
1919 J.D. Salinger, writer of the adolescent classic, *Catcher in the Rye*
Sun aspects: Pluto
Moon: Sagittarius/Capricorn   Mercury: Sagittarius
Venus: Capricorn

2 January
1969 Michael Schumacher, racing driver, twice world champion
Sun aspects: Saturn, Uranus
Moon: Gemini/Cancer   Mercury: Capricorn
Venus: Aquarius

3 January
1956 Mel Gibson, actor and director, *Braveheart*, *Mad Max*, *The Passion of the Christ*
Sun aspects: none
Moon: Virgo/Libra   Mercury: Capricorn   Venus: Aquarius

4 January
1809 Louis Braille, inventor of Braille, writing for the blind
Sun aspects: none
Moon: Leo   Mercury: Capricorn   Venus: Aquarius

5 January
1946 Diane Keaton, actress and director, *Annie Hall*
Sun aspects: Saturn, Neptune
Moon: Aquarius   Mercury: Sagittarius   Venus: Capricorn

6 January
1412 Joan of Arc, French patriot and martyr, guided by the voices of saints
Sun aspects: none
Moon: Pisces   Mercury: Capricorn   Venus: Sagittarius

7 January
1844 Saint Bernadette of Lourdes, saw visions of the Virgin Mary
Sun aspects: Pluto
Moon: Leo   Mercury: Aquarius   Venus: Aquarius

8 January
1935 Elvis Presley, singer, the king of rock 'n' roll, 'Jailhouse Rock'
Sun aspects: Pluto
Moon: Pisces   Mercury: Capricorn   Venus: Capricorn

9 January
1913 Richard Nixon, US president involved in the Watergate scandal
Sun aspects: Neptune
Moon: Aquarius   Mercury: Capricorn   Venus: Pisces

10 January
1945 Rod Stewart, much-married singer, 'Do Ya Think I'm Sexy?'
Sun aspects: none
Moon: Scorpio   Mercury: Sagittarius   Venus: Pisces

11 January
1906 Dr Albert Hofmann, researcher who accidentally discovered the psychedelic drug LSD
Sun aspects: none
Moon: Cancer/Leo   Mercury: Sagittarius
Venus: Capricorn

12 January
1628 Charles Perrault, writer of fairy tales, *Sleeping Beauty*, *Cinderella*
Sun aspects: Neptune
Moon: Pisces/Aries   Mercury: Capricorn   Venus: Aquarius

13 January
1884 Dame Sybil Hathaway, formidable feudal ruler of Sark from 1927 to 1972
Sun aspects: none
Moon: Cancer/Leo   Mercury: Aquarius   Venus: Aquarius

14 January
1875 Albert Schweitzer, medical missionary, builder of Lamborene leper hospital
Sun aspects: Neptune
Moon: Aries   Mercury: Capricorn   Venus: Sagittarius

15 January
1929 Martin Luther King, American civil-rights activist
Sun aspects: Pluto
Moon: Pisces   Mercury: Aquarius   Venus: Pisces

16 January
1974 Kate Moss, waif-like model
Sun aspects: Uranus
Moon: Scorpio   Mercury: Aquarius   Venus: Aquarius

17 January
1942 Muhammad Ali, three-times world heavyweight boxing champion
Sun aspects: Pluto
Moon: Aquarius   Mercury: Aquarius   Venus: Aquarius

18 January
1899 Al Capone, Chicago gangster and racketeer, jailed for tax evasion
Sun aspects: none
Moon: Aries   Mercury: Capricorn   Venus: Sagittarius

19 January
1943 Janis Joplin, rock star who died of a drugs overdose
Sun aspects: Pluto
Moon: Cancer   Mercury: Aquarius   Venus: Aquarius

20 January
1926 Patricia Neal, Oscar-winning actress and wife of Roald Dahl, *Hud*
Sun aspects: none
Moon: Aries   Mercury: Capricorn   Venus: Aquarius

Other Capricorn people mentioned in this book
Princess Alexandra, member of the Royal Family ☆ Mary Archer, chemist and loyal wife of Jeffrey Archer ☆ Rowan Atkinson, comedian, *Blackadder*, *Mr Bean* ☆ Joan Baez, folk singer and political activist ☆ Clara Barton, founder of the American Red Cross ☆ Shirley Bassey, singer, 'Goldfinger' ☆ Cecil Beaton, photographer of the famous ☆ Simone de Beauvoir, feminist writer, *The Second Sex* ☆ Robert Bly, poet and writer, *Iron John* ☆ Victor Borge, musician and entertainer ☆ David Bowie, musician, 'Ziggy Stardust' ☆ Tycho Brahe, astronomer ☆ Richard Briers, actor, *The Good Life* ☆ Max Bruch, composer, *Kol Nidrei* ☆ Nicolas Cage, actor, *Captain Corelli's Mandolin* ☆ Dyan Cannon, actress, *Bob & Carol & Ted & Alice* ☆ Bonnie Prince Charlie, pretender to the British throne ☆ Anthony Clare, psychiatrist, *In the Psychiatrist's Chair* ☆ Kevin Costner, actor, *Dances with Wolves* ☆ Quentin Crisp, one of the 'stately homos of England', *The Naked Civil Servant* ☆ John Delorean, car designer and entrepreneur ☆ Faye Dunaway, actress, *Bonnie and Clyde* ☆ Umberto Eco, writer, *The Name of the Rose* ☆ Marianne Faithfull, singer, 'As Tears Go By' ☆ Heidi Fleiss, Hollywood brothel-keeper ☆ E.M. Forster, writer, *A Passage to India* ☆ William Fox, founder of 20th Century Fox film studios ☆ Benjamin Franklin, scientist and statesman ☆ Sir James Frazer, anthropologist, *The Golden Bough* ☆ Joe Frazier, boxer ☆ Oliver Hardy, comedian teamed with Stan Laurel ☆ Kahlil Gibran, poet, *The Prophet* ☆ William Gladstone, Victorian statesman ☆ Hermann Goering, founder of the Gestapo ☆ Conrad Hilton, hotel-chain magnate ☆ Anthony

Hopkins, actor, *The Silence of the Lambs* ☆ William James, psychologist, *Varieties of Religious Experience* ☆ Danny Kaye, actor, *The Secret Life of Walter Mitty* ☆ Nigella Lawson, TV celebrity cook ☆ Annie Lennox, singer, 'Here Comes The Rain Again' ☆ Liz Lochhead, poet and playright, *Miseryguts*; Linda Lovelace, porn film actress, *Deep Throat* ☆ St Ignatius Loyola, founder of the Jesuit religious order ☆ Compton MacKenzie, author, *Whisky Galore* ☆ Sarah Miles, actress, *White Mischief* ☆ Henry Miller, author and guru of sexual liberation, *Tropic of Capricorn* ☆ A.A. Milne, children's author, *Winnie the Pooh* ☆ Warren Mitchell, actor, cockney bigot Alf Garnet in *Till Death Us Do Part* ☆ Molière, French playwright, *Le Misanthrope* ☆ Nostradamus, French physician and predictive astrologer, *Centuries* ☆ Aristotle Onassis, wealthy Greek ship-owner ☆ Tara Palmer-Tomkinson, 'It' girl ☆ Dolly Parton, singer and actress, *The Best Little Whorehouse in Texas* ☆ Cynthia Payne, saucy brothel-owner and writer, *Entertaining at Home* ☆ Edgar Allan Poe, author and poet, *The Murders in the Rue Morgue* ☆ Telly Savalas, actor, *Kojak* ☆ Arthur Scargill, trade union leader of the 1984 miners' national strike ☆ Del Shannon, singer, 'Runaway' ☆ Harold Shipman, GP who murdered over 200 of his elderly patients ☆ Carol Smillie, TV presenter, *Changing Rooms* ☆ Maggie Smith, actress, *The Prime of Miss Jean Brodie* ☆ Susan Sontag, US writer and critic, *Regarding the Pain of Others* ☆ Doris Stokes, medium, *Voices in my Ear* ☆ Janet Street-Porter, journalist and TV personality ☆ John Thaw, actor, *Inspector Morse* ☆ J.R.R. Tolkien, author, *The Lord of the Rings* ☆ Sophie Tucker, actress and singer, 'I'm the Last of the Red Hot Mamas' ☆ Tracey Ullman, comedienne, *The Tracey Ullman Show* ☆ Madam C.J. Walker, first black American woman millionaire ☆ Dennis Wheatley, occult and fantasy writer, *The Devil Rides Out* ☆ Alexander Woollcott, writer and wit, *The Man Who Came to Dinner* ☆ Susannah York, actress, *Tom Jones*.

ELEVEN

Finding Your Sun, Moon, Mercury and Venus Signs

ALL OF THE ASTROLOGICAL DATA IN THIS BOOK WAS CALCULATED by Astrolabe, who also supply a wide range of astrological software. I am most grateful for their help and generosity.

ASTROLABE, PO Box 1750, Brewster, MA 02631, USA www.alabe.com

PLEASE NOTE THAT ALL OF THE TIMES GIVEN ARE IN GREENWICH MEAN TIME (GMT). If you were born during British Summer Time (BST) you will need to subtract one hour from your birth time to convert it to GMT. If you were born outside of the British Isles, find the time zone of your place of birth and the number of hours it is different from GMT. Add the difference in hours if you were born west of the UK, and subtract the difference if you were born east of the UK to convert your birth time to GMT.

Your Sun Sign

Check your year of birth, and if you were born between the dates and times given the Sun was in Capricorn when you were born – confirming that you're a Capricorn. If you were born before the time on the date that Capricorn begins in your year, you are a Sagittarian. If you were born after the time on the date Capricorn ends in your year, you are an Aquarian.

Your Moon Sign

The Moon changes sign every two and a half days. To find your Moon sign, first find your year of birth. You will notice that in each year box there are three columns.

The second column shows the day of the month that the Moon changed sign, while the first column gives the abbreviation for the sign that the Moon entered on that date.

In the middle column, the month has been omitted, so that the dates run from, for example, 22 to 31 (December) and then from 1 to 21 (January).

In the third column, after the star, the time that the Moon changed sign on that day is given.

Look down the middle column of your year box to find your date of birth. If your birth date is given, look to the third column to find the time that the Moon changed sign. If you were born after that time, your Moon sign is given in the first column next to your birth date. If you were born before that time, your Moon sign is the one above the one next to your birth date.

If your birth date is not given, find the closest date before it. The sign shown next to that date is your Moon sign.

If you were born on a day that the Moon changed signs and you do not know your time of birth, try out both of that day's Moon signs and feel which one fits you best.

The abbreviations for the signs are as follows:

Aries – Ari   Taurus – Tau   Gemini – Gem   Cancer – Can
Leo – Leo   Virgo – Vir   Libra – Lib   Scorpio – Sco
Sagittarius – Sag   Capricorn – Cap   Aquarius – Aqu   Pisces – Pis

Your Mercury Sign

Find your year of birth and then the column in which your birthday falls. Look up to the top of the column to find your Mercury sign. You will see that some dates appear twice. This is because Mercury changed sign that day. If your birthday falls on one of these dates, try out both Mercury signs and see which one fits you best. If you know your birth time, you can find out for sure which Mercury sign is yours on my website – www.janeridderpatrick.com.

Your Venus Sign

Find your year of birth and then the column in which your birthday falls. Look up to the top of the column to find your Venus sign. Some dates have two possible signs. That's because Venus changed signs that day. Try them both out and see which fits you best. If the year you are interested in doesn't appear in the tables, or you have Venus in the same sign as your Sun and want to know whether you have a morning or evening star Venus, you can find the information on my website – www.janeridderpatrick.com.

♑ Capricorn Sun Tables ☉

YEAR	CAPRICORN BEGINS	CAPRICORN ENDS
1930	22 Dec 13.39	21 Jan 00.17
1931	22 Dec 19.29	21 Jan 06.06
1932	22 Dec 01.14	20 Jan 11.52
1933	22 Dec 06.57	20 Jan 23.28
1934	22 Dec 12.49	20 Jan 23.28
1935	22 Dec 18.37	21 Jan 05.12
1936	22 Dec 00.26	20 Jan 11.01
1937	22 Dec 06.21	20 Jan 16.58
1938	22 Dec 12.13	20 Jan 22.50
1939	22 Dec 18.05	21 Jan 04.44
1940	21 Dec 23.54	20 Jan 10.33
1941	22 Dec 05.44	20 Jan 16.23
1942	22 Dec 11.39	20 Jan 22.18
1943	22 Dec 17.29	21 Jan 04.07
1944	21 Dec 23.14	20 Jan 09.53
1945	22 Dec 05.03	20 Jan 15.44
1946	22 Dec 10.53	20 Jan 21.31
1947	22 Dec 16.42	21 Jan 03.18
1948	21 Dec 22.33	20 Jan 09.08
1949	22 Dec 04.22	20 Jan 14.59
1950	22 Dec 10.13	20 Jan 20.52
1951	22 Dec 16.00	21 Jan 02.38
1952	21 Dec 21.43	20 Jan 08.21
1953	22 Dec 03.31	20 Jan 14.11
1954	22 Dec 09.24	20 Jan 20.01
1955	22 Dec 15.10	21 Jan 01.48
1956	21 Dec 20.59	20 Jan 07.38
1957	22 Dec 02.48	20 Jan 13.28
1958	22 Dec 08.39	20 Jan 19.18
1959	22 Dec 14.34	21 Jan 01.10
1960	21 Dec 20.25	20 Jan 07.01
1961	22 Dec 02.19	20 Jan 12.57
1962	22 Dec 08.15	20 Jan 18.53
1963	22 Dec 14.01	21 Jan 00.41

YEAR	CAPRICORN BEGINS	CAPRICORN ENDS
1964	21 Dec 19.49	20 Jan 06.28
1965	22 Dec 01.40	20 Jan 12.19
1966	22 Dec 07.28	20 Jan 18.07
1967	22 Dec 13.16	20 Jan 23.54
1968	21 Dec 18.59	20 Jan 05.38
1969	22 Dec 00.43	20 Jan 11.23
1970	22 Dec 06.35	20 Jan 17.12
1971	22 Dec 12.23	20 Jan 22.59
1972	21 Dec 18.12	20 Jan 04.48
1973	22 Dec 00.07	20 Jan 10.45
1974	22 Dec 05.55	20 Jan 16.36
1975	22 Dec 11.45	20 Jan 22.25
1976	21 Dec 17.35	20 Jan 04.14
1977	21 Dec 23.23	20 Jan 10.03
1978	22 Dec 05.20	20 Jan 15.59
1979	22 Dec 11.09	20 Jan 21.48
1980	21 Dec 16.56	20 Jan 03.36
1981	21 Dec 22.50	20 Jan 09.30
1982	22 Dec 04.38	20 Jan 15.16
1983	22 Dec 10.29	20 Jan 21.05
1984	21 Dec 16.22	20 Jan 02.57
1985	21 Dec 22.07	20 Jan 08.46
1986	22 Dec 04.02	20 Jan 14.40
1987	22 Dec 09.45	20 Jan 20.24
1988	21 Dec 15.27	20 Jan 02.07
1989	21 Dec 21.21	20 Jan 08.01
1990	22 Dec 03.07	20 Jan 13.47
1991	22 Dec 08.53	20 Jan 19.32
1992	21 Dec 14.43	20 Jan 01.22
1993	21 Dec 20.25	20 Jan 07.07
1994	22 Dec 02.22	20 Jan 13.00
1995	22 Dec 08.16	20 Jan 18.52
1996	21 Dec 14.05	20 Jan 00.42
1997	21 Dec 20.06	20 Jan 06.46
1998	22 Dec 01.56	20 Jan 12.37
1999	22 Dec 07.43	20 Jan 18.23
2000	21 Dec 13.37	20 Jan 00.17

♑ Capricorn – Finding Your Moon Sign ☽

1930–1		
Aqu	22	*15:43
Pis	25	*03:35
Ari	27	*16:29
Tau	30	*03:50
Gem	1	*11:32
Can	3	*15:20
Leo	5	*16:31
Vir	7	*17:06
Lib	9	*18:48
Sco	11	*22:41
Sag	14	*04:50
Cap	16	*13:02
Aqu	18	*23:04

1931–2		
Tau	19	*23:44
Gem	22	*10:58
Can	24	*19:21
Leo	27	*01:15
Vir	29	*05:40
Lib	31	*09:17
Sco	2	*12:23
Sag	4	*15:15
Cap	6	*18:37
Aqu	8	*23:44
Pis	11	*07:49
Ari	13	*19:07
Tau	16	*08:02
Gem	18	*19:46

1932–3		
Sco	23	*01:51
Sag	25	*02:41
Cap	27	*02:31
Aqu	29	*03:23
Pis	31	*07:16
Ari	2	*15:14
Tau	5	*02:36
Gem	7	*15:19
Can	10	*03:15
Leo	12	*13:25
Vir	14	*21:41
Lib	17	*04:02
Sco	19	*08:23

1933–4		
Pis	21	*12:16
Ari	23	*17:15
Tau	26	*01:43
Gem	28	*12:43
Can	31	*01:06
Leo	2	*13:55
Vir	5	*02:08
Lib	7	*12:19
Sco	9	*19:10
Sag	11	*22:16
Cap	13	*22:36
Aqu	15	*21:56
Pis	17	*22:18

1934–5		
Can	21	*00:11
Leo	23	*11:37
Vir	26	*00:31
Lib	28	*12:58
Sco	30	*22:39
Sag	2	*04:26
Cap	4	*06:43
Aqu	6	*07:03
Pis	8	*07:17
Ari	10	*09:03
Tau	12	*13:25
Gem	14	*20:43
Can	17	*06:37
Leo	19	*18:26

♑ Capricorn – Finding Your Moon Sign ☽

1935–6		
Sag	23	*05:44
Cap	25	*12:26
Aqu	27	*16:45
Pis	29	*19:41
Ari	31	*22:15
Tau	3	*01:11
Gem	5	*05:04
Can	7	*10:29
Leo	9	*18:01
Vir	12	*04:05
Lib	14	*16:10
Sco	17	*04:38
Sag	19	*15:10

1936–7		
Ari	21	*12:25
Tau	23	*15:05
Gem	25	*16:24
Can	27	*17:36
Leo	29	*20:14
Vir	1	*01:46
Lib	3	*10:55
Sco	5	*22:58
Sag	8	*11:42
Cap	10	*22:52
Aqu	13	*07:24
Pis	15	*13:27
Ari	17	*17:48
Tau	19	*21:06

1937–8		
Vir	22	*03:57
Lib	24	*09:54
Sco	26	*19:44
Sag	29	*08:11
Cap	31	*21:16
Aqu	3	*09:30
Pis	5	*20:06
Ari	8	*04:28
Tau	10	*10:04
Gem	12	*12:49
Can	14	*13:21
Leo	16	*13:09
Vir	18	*14:13

1938–9		
Cap	21	*19:38
Aqu	24	*07:58
Pis	26	*20:40
Ari	29	*08:13
Tau	31	*16:46
Gem	2	*21:18
Can	4	*22:19
Leo	6	*21:32
Vir	8	*21:08
Lib	10	*23:12
Sco	13	*04:54
Sag	15	*14:10
Cap	18	*01:43

1939–40		
Tau	21	*16:31
Gem	24	*00:35
Can	26	*05:02
Leo	28	*07:04
Vir	30	*08:28
Lib	1	*10:44
Sco	3	*14:36
Sag	5	*20:12
Cap	8	*03:30
Aqu	10	*12:42
Pis	13	*00:03
Ari	15	*12:55
Tau	18	*01:14

♑ Capricorn – Finding Your Moon Sign ☽

1940–1

Lib	22	*01:36
Sco	24	*04:29
Sag	26	*06:36
Cap	28	*08:58
Aqu	30	*13:09
Pis	1	*20:35
Ari	4	*07:34
Tau	6	*20:28
Gem	9	*08:26
Can	11	*17:33
Leo	13	*23:38
Vir	16	*03:45
Lib	18	*06:59

1941–2

Pis	22	*20:33
Ari	25	*04:24
Tau	27	*15:43
Gem	30	*04:27
Can	1	*16:41
Leo	4	*03:32
Vir	6	*12:41
Lib	8	*19:47
Sco	11	*00:23
Sag	13	*02:30
Cap	15	*03:06
Aqu	17	*03:52
Pis	19	*06:43

1942–3

Can	22	*14:45
Leo	25	*03:35
Vir	27	*16:09
Lib	30	*02:43
Sco	1	*09:38
Sag	3	*12:32
Cap	5	*12:34
Aqu	7	*11:42
Pis	9	*12:04
Ari	11	*15:21
Tau	13	*22:22
Gem	16	*08:39
Can	18	*20:53

1943–4

Sco	22	*11:44
Sag	24	*17:43
Cap	26	*20:23
Aqu	28	*21:20
Pis	30	*22:17
Ari	2	*00:34
Tau	4	*04:58
Gem	6	*11:44
Can	8	*20:48
Leo	11	*07:57
Vir	13	*20:38
Lib	16	*09:28
Sco	18	*20:26

1944–5

Ari	22	*14:42
Tau	24	*17:24
Gem	26	*20:26
Can	29	*00:44
Leo	31	*07:19
Vir	2	*16:49
Lib	5	*04:43
Sco	7	*17:12
Sag	10	*03:54
Cap	12	*11:26
Aqu	14	*15:56
Pis	16	*18:27
Ari	18	*20:20

♑ Capricorn – Finding Your Moon Sign ☽

1945–6		
Leo	21	*09:31
Vir	23	*14:44
Lib	25	*23:45
Sco	28	*11:43
Sag	31	*00:31
Cap	2	*12:10
Aqu	4	*21:37
Pis	7	*04:46
Ari	9	*09:55
Tau	11	*13:24
Gem	13	*15:42
Can	15	*17:32
Leo	17	*20:03

1946–7		
Cap	23	*10:50
Aqu	25	*23:29
Pis	28	*10:42
Ari	30	*19:30
Tau	2	*01:04
Gem	4	*03:25
Can	6	*03:27
Leo	8	*02:53
Vir	10	*03:45
Lib	12	*07:54
Sco	14	*16:15
Sag	17	*04:03
Cap	19	*17:10

1947–8		
Tau	23	*06:11
Gem	25	*10:45
Can	27	*12:02
Leo	29	*11:41
Vir	31	*11:47
Lib	2	*14:11
Sco	4	*19:51
Sag	7	*04:40
Cap	9	*15:41
Aqu	12	*03:54
Pis	14	*16:35
Ari	17	*04:43
Tau	19	*14:41

1948–9		
Vir	21	*00:19
Lib	23	*02:59
Sco	25	*06:38
Sag	27	*11:29
Cap	29	*17:46
Aqu	1	*02:08
Pis	3	*12:58
Ari	6	*01:40
Tau	8	*14:02
Gem	10	*23:29
Can	13	*04:56
Leo	15	*07:07
Vir	17	*07:52
Lib	19	*09:03

1949–50		
Aqu	22	*02:25
Pis	24	*09:20
Ari	26	*20:04
Tau	29	*08:57
Gem	31	*21:12
Can	3	*06:55
Leo	5	*13:57
Vir	7	*19:05
Lib	9	*23:07
Sco	12	*02:27
Sag	14	*05:16
Cap	16	*08:06
Aqu	18	*12:07

♑ Capricorn – Finding Your Moon Sign ☽

1950–1		
Gem	21	*17:49
Can	24	*06:17
Leo	26	*17:45
Vir	29	*03:40
Lib	31	*11:18
Sco	2	*15:57
Sag	4	*17:38
Cap	6	*17:31
Aqu	8	*17:35
Pis	10	*19:56
Ari	13	*02:06
Tau	15	*12:11
Gem	18	*00:35

1951–2		
Lib	21	*16:40
Sco	23	*23:36
Sag	26	*02:25
Cap	28	*02:23
Aqu	30	*01:36
Pis	1	*02:11
Ari	3	*05:41
Tau	5	*12:44
Gem	7	*22:42
Can	10	*10:34
Leo	12	*23:19
Vir	15	*11:59
Lib	17	*23:18

1952–3		
Pis	21	*13:45
Ari	23	*16:30
Tau	25	*20:46
Gem	28	*02:48
Can	30	*10:53
Leo	1	*21:17
Vir	4	*09:40
Lib	6	*22:35
Sco	9	*09:42
Sag	11	*17:13
Cap	13	*20:54
Aqu	15	*21:56
Pis	17	*22:07
Ari	19	*23:09

1953–4		
Leo	22	*20:23
Vir	25	*05:24
Lib	27	*17:10
Sco	30	*05:42
Sag	1	*16:39
Cap	4	*00:44
Aqu	6	*06:08
Pis	8	*09:42
Ari	10	*12:26
Tau	12	*15:09
Gem	14	*18:29
Can	16	*23:01
Leo	19	*05:24

1954–5		
Sag	22	*13:34
Cap	25	*01:39
Aqu	27	*11:59
Pis	29	*20:08
Ari	1	*01:55
Tau	3	*05:23
Gem	5	*07:04
Can	7	*08:00
Leo	9	*09:41
Vir	11	*13:43
Lib	13	*21:15
Sco	16	*08:14
Sag	18	*21:01

♑ Capricorn – Finding Your Moon Sign ☽

1955–6		
Ari	22	*10:04
Tau	24	*15:32
Gem	26	*17:32
Can	28	*17:17
Leo	30	*16:36
Vir	1	*17:30
Lib	3	*21:45
Sco	6	*05:59
Sag	8	*17:32
Cap	11	*06:33
Aqu	13	*19:19
Pis	16	*06:47
Ari	18	*16:16

1956–7		
Vir	22	*02:56
Lib	24	*05:38
Sco	26	*11:09
Sag	28	*19:20
Cap	31	*05:36
Aqu	2	*17:24
Pis	5	*06:04
Ari	7	*18:22
Tau	10	*04:25
Gem	12	*10:42
Can	14	*13:04
Leo	16	*12:50
Vir	18	*12:04

1957–8		
Cap	21	*07:47
Aqu	23	*15:19
Pis	26	*01:41
Ari	28	*14:12
Tau	31	*02:36
Gem	2	*12:19
Can	4	*18:21
Leo	6	*21:20
Vir	8	*22:58
Lib	11	*00:52
Sco	13	*04:02
Sag	15	*08:49
Cap	17	*15:13
Aqu	19	*23:22

1958–9		
Gem	23	*10:08
Can	25	*20:32
Leo	28	*04:32
Vir	30	*10:40
Lib	1	*15:20
Sco	3	*18:41
Sag	5	*20:55
Cap	7	*22:50
Aqu	10	*01:52
Pis	12	*07:40
Ari	14	*17:09
Tau	17	*05:32
Gem	19	*18:15

1959–60		
Lib	23	*02:27
Sco	25	*07:00
Sag	27	*08:15
Cap	29	*07:37
Aqu	31	*07:15
Pis	2	*09:20
Ari	4	*15:22
Tau	7	*01:23
Gem	9	*13:45
Can	12	*02:23
Leo	14	*13:58
Vir	17	*00:02
Lib	19	*08:13

103

♑ Capricorn – Finding Your Moon Sign ☽

1960–1		
Pis	22	*16:47
Ari	24	*20:35
Tau	27	*03:30
Gem	29	*13:01
Can	1	*00:21
Leo	3	*12:53
Vir	6	*01:47
Lib	8	*13:30
Sco	10	*22:07
Sag	13	*02:39
Cap	15	*03:40
Aqu	17	*02:55
Pis	19	*02:32

1961–2		
Can	22	*00:50
Leo	24	*10:26
Vir	26	*22:29
Lib	29	*11:25
Sco	31	*22:40
Sag	3	*06:22
Cap	5	*10:22
Aqu	7	*11:59
Pis	9	*12:53
Ari	11	*14:34
Tau	13	*18:01
Gem	15	*23:42
Can	18	*07:39

1962–3		
Sco	21	*18:17
Sag	24	*05:32
Cap	26	*14:17
Aqu	28	*20:41
Pis	31	*01:19
Ari	2	*04:47
Tau	4	*07:33
Gem	6	*10:14
Can	8	*13:41
Leo	10	*19:01
Vir	13	*03:07
Lib	15	*14:04
Sco	18	*02:35

1963–4		
Pis	21	*11:27
Ari	23	*17:40
Tau	25	*20:56
Gem	27	*21:57
Can	29	*22:07
Leo	31	*23:10
Vir	3	*02:48
Lib	5	*10:10
Sco	7	*21:04
Sag	10	*09:48
Cap	12	*22:13
Aqu	15	*08:47
Pis	17	*17:03
Ari	19	*23:09

1964–5		
Leo	21	*06:30
Vir	23	*07:42
Lib	25	*12:05
Sco	27	*20:11
Sag	30	*07:20
Cap	1	*20:06
Aqu	4	*09:03
Pis	6	*21:05
Ari	9	*07:07
Tau	11	*14:09
Gem	13	*17:48
Can	15	*18:34
Leo	17	*17:57
Vir	19	*17:54

♑ Capricorn – Finding Your Moon Sign ☽

1965–6		
Cap	22	*19:26
Aqu	25	*06:44
Pis	27	*19:17
Ari	30	*07:39
Tau	1	*17:45
Gem	4	*00:04
Can	6	*02:39
Leo	8	*02:49
Vir	10	*02:34
Lib	12	*03:53
Sco	14	*08:09
Sag	16	*15:40
Cap	19	*01:45

1966–7		
Tau	22	*15:06
Gem	25	*01:12
Can	27	*07:57
Leo	29	*11:56
Vir	31	*14:32
Lib	2	*17:03
Sco	4	*20:16
Sag	7	*00:28
Cap	9	*05:53
Aqu	11	*13:06
Pis	13	*22:45
Ari	16	*10:48
Tau	18	*23:38

1967–8		
Vir	22	*02:20
Lib	24	*07:26
Sco	26	*10:35
Sag	28	*12:08
Cap	30	*13:11
Aqu	1	*15:24
Pis	3	*20:36
Ari	6	*05:45
Tau	8	*18:02
Gem	11	*06:54
Can	13	*17:53
Leo	16	*02:08
Vir	18	*08:10

1968–9		
Aqu	21	*21:00
Pis	23	*23:02
Ari	26	*05:02
Tau	28	*14:57
Gem	31	*03:10
Can	2	*15:52
Leo	5	*03:54
Vir	7	*14:41
Lib	9	*23:31
Sco	12	*05:31
Sag	14	*08:18
Cap	16	*08:38
Aqu	18	*08:17

1969–70		
Gem	21	*03:28
Can	23	*14:08
Leo	26	*02:21
Vir	28	*15:19
Lib	31	*03:17
Sco	2	*12:01
Sag	4	*16:32
Cap	6	*17:29
Aqu	8	*16:47
Pis	10	*16:36
Ari	12	*18:48
Tau	15	*00:21
Gem	17	*09:07
Can	19	*20:13

VB Capricorn – Finding Your Moon Sign ☽

1970–1

Lib	21	*00:00
Sco	23	*11:25
Sag	25	*19:26
Cap	28	*00:00
Aqu	30	*02:23
Pis	1	*04:07
Ari	3	*06:26
Tau	5	*10:00
Gem	7	*15:08
Can	9	*22:09
Leo	12	*07:24
Vir	14	*18:57
Lib	17	*07:52
Sco	19	*20:03

1971–2

Pis	22	*17:09
Ari	24	*21:08
Tau	26	*23:44
Gem	29	*01:38
Can	31	*04:01
Leo	2	*08:22
Vir	4	*15:50
Lib	7	*02:33
Sco	9	*15:03
Sag	12	*02:56
Cap	14	*12:24
Aqu	16	*19:03
Pis	18	*23:27

1972–3

Leo	22	*12:35
Vir	24	*16:03
Lib	26	*23:22
Sco	29	*10:10
Sag	31	*22:51
Cap	3	*11:29
Aqu	5	*22:46
Pis	8	*08:02
Ari	10	*14:56
Tau	12	*19:24
Gem	14	*21:40
Can	16	*22:38
Leo	18	*23:40

1973–4

Sag	21	*21:20
Cap	24	*09:41
Aqu	26	*22:42
Pis	29	*11:09
Ari	31	*21:32
Tau	3	*04:37
Gem	5	*07:59
Can	7	*08:27
Leo	9	*07:42
Vir	11	*07:41
Lib	13	*10:22
Sco	15	*16:54
Sag	18	*03:12

1974–5

Ari	21	*20:34
Tau	24	*06:44
Gem	26	*13:14
Can	28	*16:14
Leo	30	*17:04
Vir	1	*17:32
Lib	3	*19:21
Sco	5	*23:39
Sag	8	*06:39
Cap	10	*15:58
Aqu	13	*03:03
Pis	15	*15:23
Ari	18	*04:03

♑ Capricorn – Finding Your Moon Sign ☽

1975–6		
Leo	21	*02:53
Vir	23	*06:27
Lib	25	*09:27
Sco	27	*12:27
Sag	29	*15:52
Cap	31	*20:16
Aqu	3	*02:33
Pis	5	*11:35
Ari	7	*23:21
Tau	10	*12:08
Gem	12	*23:18
Can	15	*06:59
Leo	17	*11:14
Vir	19	*13:24

1976–7		
Cap	21	*03:11
Aqu	23	*04:48
Pis	25	*09:37
Ari	27	*18:31
Tau	30	*06:43
Gem	1	*19:42
Can	4	*07:11
Leo	6	*16:20
Vir	8	*23:22
Lib	11	*04:47
Sco	13	*08:43
Sag	15	*11:17
Cap	17	*13:01
Aqu	19	*15:12

1977–8		
Gem	22	*16:51
Can	25	*05:29
Leo	27	*17:51
Vir	30	*05:13
Lib	1	*14:30
Sco	3	*20:33
Sag	5	*23:02
Cap	7	*22:54
Aqu	9	*22:05
Pis	11	*22:51
Ari	14	*03:05
Tau	16	*11:31
Gem	18	*23:06

1978–9		
Lib	22	*16:39
Sco	25	*01:30
Sag	27	*06:07
Cap	29	*07:15
Aqu	31	*06:52
Pis	2	*07:08
Ari	4	*09:42
Tau	6	*15:18
Gem	8	*23:43
Can	11	*10:14
Leo	13	*22:16
Vir	16	*11:09
Lib	18	*23:39

1979–80		
Aqu	21	*17:12
Pis	23	*19:50
Ari	25	*22:40
Tau	28	*02:07
Gem	30	*06:32
Can	1	*12:29
Leo	3	*20:47
Vir	6	*07:48
Lib	8	*20:37
Sco	11	*08:54
Sag	13	*18:16
Cap	15	*23:49
Aqu	18	*02:24

♑ Capricorn – Finding Your Moon Sign ☽

1980–1

Can	21	*18:02
Leo	23	*21:34
Vir	26	*04:32
Lib	28	*15:05
Sco	31	*03:35
Sag	2	*15:41
Cap	5	*01:40
Aqu	7	*09:11
Pis	9	*14:41
Ari	11	*18:43
Tau	13	*21:44
Gem	16	*00:17
Can	18	*03:07

1981–2

Sag	23	*12:11
Cap	26	*00:58
Aqu	28	*12:52
Pis	30	*22:59
Ari	2	*06:32
Tau	4	*11:01
Gem	6	*12:47
Can	8	*13:01
Leo	10	*13:21
Vir	12	*15:37
Lib	14	*21:17
Sco	17	*06:46
Sag	19	*19:00

1982–3

Pis	21	*00:55
Ari	23	*11:32
Tau	25	*18:36
Gem	27	*21:47
Can	29	*22:11
Leo	31	*21:33
Vir	2	*21:50
Lib	5	*00:45
Sco	7	*07:16
Sag	9	*17:13
Cap	12	*05:25
Aqu	14	*18:26
Pis	17	*07:02
Ari	19	*18:07

1983–4

Leo	22	*07:43
Vir	24	*09:01
Lib	26	*11:19
Sco	28	*15:27
Sag	30	*21:44
Cap	2	*06:07
Aqu	4	*16:30
Pis	7	*04:34
Ari	9	*17:15
Tau	12	*04:35
Gem	14	*12:38
Can	16	*16:46
Leo	18	*17:49

1984–5

Cap	22	*10:21
Aqu	24	*15:47
Pis	27	*00:19
Ari	29	*11:49
Tau	1	*00:35
Gem	3	*11:59
Can	5	*20:16
Leo	8	*01:27
Vir	10	*04:39
Lib	12	*07:13
Sco	14	*10:07
Sag	16	*13:48
Cap	18	*18:28

♑ Capricorn – Finding Your Moon Sign ☽

1985–6		
Tau	21	*19:40
Gem	24	*08:44
Can	26	*20:43
Leo	29	*06:44
Vir	31	*14:42
Lib	2	*20:44
Sco	5	*00:43
Sag	7	*02:46
Cap	9	*03:41
Aqu	11	*05:01
Pis	13	*08:39
Ari	15	*16:03
Tau	18	*03:13

1986–7		
Vir	21	*19:30
Lib	24	*05:04
Sco	26	*11:04
Sag	28	*13:18
Cap	30	*12:53
Aqu	1	*11:54
Pis	3	*12:37
Ari	5	*16:51
Tau	8	*01:13
Gem	10	*12:39
Can	13	*01:18
Leo	15	*13:44
Vir	18	*01:14

1987–8		
Aqu	22	*21:20
Pis	24	*22:10
Ari	27	*01:06
Tau	29	*06:36
Gem	31	*14:29
Can	3	*00:17
Leo	5	*11:47
Vir	8	*00:35
Lib	10	*13:16
Sco	12	*23:37
Sag	15	*05:58
Cap	17	*08:14
Aqu	19	*08:01

1988–9		
Can	23	*02:35
Leo	25	*09:58
Vir	27	*20:27
Lib	30	*09:09
Sco	1	*21:32
Sag	4	*07:11
Cap	6	*13:12
Aqu	8	*16:30
Pis	10	*18:30
Ari	12	*20:35
Tau	14	*23:36
Gem	17	*03:56
Can	19	*09:57

1989–90		
Sco	22	*16:18
Sag	25	*04:36
Cap	27	*15:09
Aqu	29	*23:36
Pis	1	*06:10
Ari	3	*10:55
Tau	5	*14:03
Gem	7	*16:01
Can	9	*17:51
Leo	11	*21:03
Vir	14	*02:58
Lib	16	*12:18
Sco	19	*00:16

♑ Capricorn – Finding Your Moon Sign ☽

1990–1		
Pis	22	*13:46
Ari	24	*21:43
Tau	27	*02:07
Gem	29	*03:25
Can	31	*03:02
Leo	2	*02:54
Vir	4	*04:57
Lib	6	*10:34
Sco	8	*19:59
Sag	11	*08:06
Cap	13	*20:59
Aqu	16	*09:03
Pis	18	*19:22

1991–2		
Can	21	*11:54
Leo	23	*11:38
Vir	25	*12:24
Lib	27	*15:38
Sco	29	*22:04
Sag	1	*07:30
Cap	3	*19:09
Aqu	6	*07:59
Pis	8	*20:51
Ari	11	*08:21
Tau	13	*16:59
Gem	15	*21:53
Can	17	*23:25
Leo	19	*22:56

1992–3		
Sag	21	*12:43
Cap	23	*20:04
Aqu	26	*05:43
Pis	28	*17:27
Ari	31	*06:06
Tau	2	*17:29
Gem	5	*01:40
Can	7	*06:10
Leo	9	*07:49
Vir	11	*08:20
Lib	13	*09:30
Sco	15	*12:42
Sag	17	*18:30

1993–4		
Ari	21	*00:19
Tau	23	*13:04
Gem	26	*00:44
Can	28	*09:45
Leo	30	*15:58
Vir	1	*20:14
Lib	3	*23:30
Sco	6	*02:28
Sag	8	*05:33
Cap	10	*09:16
Aqu	12	*14:25
Pis	14	*22:04
Ari	17	*08:42
Tau	19	*21:21

1994–5		
Vir	23	*06:00
Lib	25	*12:26
Sco	27	*16:16
Sag	29	*17:45
Cap	31	*17:57
Aqu	2	*18:38
Pis	4	*21:50
Ari	7	*04:56
Tau	9	*15:58
Gem	12	*04:57
Can	14	*17:19
Leo	17	*03:35
Vir	19	*11:38

♑ Capricorn – Finding Your Moon Sign ☽

1995-6			1996-7			1997-8			1998-9			1999-2000			2000-01		
Cap	22	*02:45	Gem	22	*05:17	Lib	21	*21:34	Aqu	21	*14:16	Can	22	*16:52	Sag	22	*21:57
Aqu	24	*01:52	Can	24	*14:14	Sco	24	*10:06	Pis	23	*21:44	Leo	24	*16:32	Cap	25	*08:53
Pis	26	*02:45	Leo	27	*01:09	Sag	26	*20:06	Ari	26	*03:02	Vir	26	*18:34	Aqu	27	*21:25
Ari	28	*07:06	Vir	29	*13:44	Cap	29	*02:47	Tau	28	*06:04	Lib	29	*00:15	Pis	30	*10:26
Tau	30	*15:21	Lib	1	*02:31	Aqu	31	*06:58	Gem	30	*07:21	Sco	31	*09:37	Ari	1	*22:13
Gem	2	*02:29	Sco	3	*13:00	Pis	2	*09:55	Can	1	*08:15	Sag	2	*21:31	Tau	4	*06:56
Can	4	*14:55	Sag	5	*19:26	Ari	4	*12:43	Leo	3	*10:31	Cap	5	*10:23	Gem	6	*11:42
Leo	7	*03:30	Cap	7	*21:53	Tau	6	*15:52	Vir	5	*15:49	Aqu	7	*22:52	Can	8	*13:07
Vir	9	*15:28	Aqu	9	*21:59	Gem	8	*19:42	Lib	8	*00:53	Pis	10	*09:58	Leo	10	*12:43
Lib	12	*01:54	Pis	11	*21:51	Can	11	*00:43	Sco	10	*12:48	Ari	12	*18:48	Vir	12	*12:26
Sco	14	*09:28	Ari	13	*23:22	Leo	13	*07:45	Sag	13	*01:22	Tau	15	*00:36	Lib	14	*14:06
Sag	16	*13:23	Tau	16	*03:40	Vir	15	*17:31	Cap	15	*12:27	Gem	17	*03:24	Sco	16	*19:02
Cap	18	*14:06	Gem	18	*10:53	Lib	18	*05:44	Aqu	17	*21:10	Can	19	*04:00	Sag	19	*03:36

⛢ Capricorn Mercury Signs ☿

YEAR	SAGITTARIUS	CAPRICORN	AQUARIUS
1930		21 Dec–20 Jan	
1931	21 Dec–14 Jan	14 Jan–20 Jan	
1932		21 Dec–20 Jan	
1933	21 Dec–1 Jan	1 Jan–20 Jan	
1934	21 Dec–25 Dec	25 Dec–13 Jan	13 Jan–20 Jan
1935		21 Dec–6 Jan	6 Jan–20 Jan
1936		21 Dec–1 Jan	1 Jan–9 Jan
		9 Jan–20 Jan	
1937	6 Jan–12 Jan	21 Dec–6 Jan	
		12 Jan–20 Jan	
1938	21 Dec–12 Jan	12 Jan–20 Jan	
1939	21 Dec–6 Jan	6 Jan–20 Jan	
1940	21 Dec–29 Dec	29 Dec–16 Jan	16 Jan–20 Jan
1941		22 Dec–9 Jan	9 Jan–20 Jan
1942		21 Dec–3 Jan	3 Jan–20 Jan
1943		21 Dec–20 Jan	
1944	23 Dec–14 Jan	21 Dec–23 Dec	
		14 Jan–20 Jan	
1945	21 Dec–9 Jan	9 Jan–20 Jan	
1946	21 Dec–3 Jan	3 Jan–20 Jan	
1947	21 Dec–26 Dec	26 Dec–14 Jan	14 Jan–20 Jan
1948		21 Dec–6 Jan	6 Jan–20 Jan
1949		21 Dec–1 Jan	1 Jan–15 Jan
		15 Jan–20 Jan	
1950		21 Dec–20 Jan	
1951	21 Dec–13 Jan	13 Jan–20 Jan	
1952	21 Dec–6 Jan	6 Jan–20 Jan	
1953	21 Dec–30 Dec	30 Dec–18 Jan	18 Jan–20 Jan
1954	21 Dec–23 Dec	23 Dec–10 Jan	10 Jan–20 Jan

YEAR	SAGITTARIUS	CAPRICORN	AQUARIUS
1955		21 Dec–4 Jan	4 Jan–20 Jan
1956		21 Dec–20 Jan	
1957		21 Dec–28 Dec	28 Dec–14 Jan
		14 Jan–20 Jan	
1958	21 Dec–10 Jan	10 Jan–20 Jan	
1959	21 Dec–4 Jan	4 Jan–20 Jan	
1960	21 Dec–27 Dec	27 Dec- 20 Jan	
1961		21 Dec–7 Jan	7 Jan–20 Jan
1962		21 Dec–13 Jan	13 Jan–20 Jan
1963		21 Dec–20 Jan	
1964	21 Dec–13 Jan	13 Jan–20 Jan	
1965	21 Dec–7 Jan	7 Jan–20 Jan	
1966	22 Dec–1 Jan	1 Jan–19 Jan	19 Jan–20 Jan
1967	21 Dec–24 Dec	24 Dec–12 Jan	12 Jan–20 Jan
1968		21 Dec–4 Jan	4 Jan–20 Jan
1969		21 Dec–20 Jan	
1970	3 Jan–14 Jan	21 Dec–3 Jan	
		14 Jan–20 Jan	
1971	21 Dec–11 Jan	11 Jan–20 Jan	
1972	21 Dec–4 Jan	4 Jan–20 Jan	
1973	21 Dec–28 Dec	28 Dec–16 Jan	16 Jan–20 Jan
1974	21 Dec–8 Jan	8 Jan–20 Jan	
1975		21 Dec–2 Jan	2 Jan–20 Jan
1976		21 Dec–20 Jan	
1977	21 Dec–13 Jan	13 Jan–20 Jan	
1978	21 Dec–8 Jan	8 Jan–20 Jan	
1979	21 Dec–2 Jan	2 Jan–20 Jan	
1980	21 Dec–25 Dec	25 Dec–12 Jan	12 Jan–20 Jan
1981		21 Dec–5 Jan	5 Jan–20 Jan
1982		21 Dec–1 Jan	1 Jan–12 Jan
		12 Jan–20 Jan	
1983		21 Dec–20 Jan	

113

YEAR	SAGITTARIUS	CAPRICORN	AQUARIUS
1984	21 Dec–11 Jan	11 Jan–20 Jan	
1985	21 Dec–5 Jan	5 Jan–20 Jan	
1986	21 Dec–29 Dec	29 Dec–17 Jan	17 Jan–20 Jan
1987	22 Dec	22 Dec–10 Jan	10 Jan–20 Jan
1988		21 Dec–2 Jan	2 Jan–20 Jan
1989		21 Dec–20 Jan	
1990	25 Dec–14 Jan	21 Dec–25 Dec	
		14 Jan–20 Jan	
1991	21 Dec -10 Jan	10 Jan–20 Jan	
1992	21 Dec–2 Jan	2 Jan–20 Jan	
1993	21 Dec–26 Dec	26 Dec–14 Jan	14 Jan–20 Jan
1994		21 Dec–6 Jan	6 Jan–20 Jan
1995		21 Dec–1 Jan	1 Jan–17 Jan
		17 Jan–20 Jan	
1996		21 Dec–20 Jan	
1997	21 Dec–12 Jan	12 Jan–20 Jan	
1998	21 Dec–7 Jan	7 Jan–20 Jan	
1999	21 Dec–31 Dec	31 Dec–18 Jan	18 Jan–20 Jan
2000	21 Dec–23 Dec	23 Dec–10 Jan	10 Jan–20 Jan

♑ Capricorn Venus Signs ♀

YEAR	SCORPIO	SAGITTARIUS	CAPRICORN	AQUARIUS	PISCES
1930	21 Dec–3 Jan	3 Jan–20 Jan			
1931		21 Dec–14 Jan	21 Dec–25 Dec	25 Dec–19 Jan	19 Jan–21 Jan
1932			14 Jan–20 Jan		
1933				21 Dec–20 Jan	
1934			21 Dec–8 Jan	8 Jan–19 Jan	
1935	21 Dec–3 Jan	3 Jan–20 Jan			
1936				21 Dec–6 Jan	6 Jan–20 Jan
1937		21 Dec–30 Dec	30 Dec–20 Jan		
1938	21 Dec–4 Jan	4 Jan–20 Jan			
1939		21 Dec–13 Jan	21 Dec–25 Dec	25 Dec–18 Jan	18 Jan–20 Jan
1940			13 Jan–20 Jan		
1941				21 Dec–20 Jan	
1942			21 Dec–8 Jan	8 Jan–20 Jan	
1943	21 Dec–3 Jan	3 Jan–20 Jan			
1944				21 Dec–5 Jan	5 Jan–20 Jan
1945		21 Dec–30 Dec	30 Dec–20 Jan		

YEAR	SCORPIO	SAGITTARIUS	CAPRICORN	AQUARIUS	PISCES
1946	21 Dec–5 Jan	5 Jan–20 Jan	21 Dec–245 Dec	24 Dec–18 Jan	18 Jan–20 Jan
1947		21 Dec–13 Jan			
1948			13 Jan–20 Jan		
1949				21 Dec–20 Jan	
1950			21 Dec–20 Jan		
1951	21 Dec–2 Jan	2 Jan–20 Jan		21 Dec–5 Jan	5 Jan–20 Jan
1952			29 Dec–20 Jan		
1953		21 Dec–29 Dec			
1954	21 Dec–6 Jan	6 Jan–20 Jan			
1955			21 Dec–24 Dec	24 Dec–17 Jan	17 Jan–20 Jan
1956		21 Dec–12 Jan	12 Jan–20 Jan		
1957				21 Dec–20 Jan	
1958			21 Dec–7 Jan	7 Jan–20 Jan	
1959	21 Dec–2 Jan	2 Jan–20 Jan		21 Dec–5 Jan	5 Jan–20 Jan
1960			29 Dec–20 Jan		
1961		21 Dec–29 Dec			
1962	21 Dec–6 Jan	6 Jan–20 Jan			
1963			21 Dec–23 Dec	23 Dec–17 Jan	17 Jan–20 Jan
1964		21 Dec–12 Jan	12 Jan–20 Jan		

YEAR	SCORPIO	SAGITTARIUS	CAPRICORN	AQUARIUS	PISCES
1965			21 Dec–6 Jan	21 Dec–20 Jan	
1966				6 Jan–20 Jan	
1967	21 Dec–1 Jan	1 Jan–20 Jan		21 Dec–4 Jan	4 Jan–20 Jan
1968					
1969		21 Dec–28 Dec	28 Dec–20 Jan		
1970	21 Dec–7 Jan	7 Jan–20 Jan			
1971		21 Dec–11 Jan	21 Dec–23 Dec	23 Dec–16 Jan	16 Jan–20 Jan
1972			11 Jan–20 Jan		
1973				21 Dec–20 Jan	
1974			21 Dec–6 Jan	6 Jan–20 Jan	
1975	21 Dec–1 Jan	1 Jan–20 Jan		21 Dec–4 Jan	4 Jan–20 Jan
1976		21 Dec–27 Dec	27 Dec–20 Jan		
1977					
1978	21 Dec–7 Jan	7 Jan–20 Jan			
1979			21 Dec–11 Jan	11 Jan–20 Jan	
1980		21 Dec–5 Jan	5 Jan–20 Jan		
1981				21 Dec–20 Jan	
1982		21 Dec–5 Jan	5 Jan–20 Jan		
1983	21 Dec–1 Jan	1 Jan–20 Jan			

YEAR	SCORPIO	SAGITTARIUS	CAPRICORN	AQUARIUS	PISCES
1984		21 Dec–27 Dec	27 Dec–20 Jan	21 Dec–4 Jan	4 Jan–20 Jan
1985	21 Dec–7 Jan	7 Jan–20 Jan			
1986					
1987		21 Dec–10 Jan		22 Dec–15 Jan	15 Jan–20 Jan
1988			10 Jan–20 Jan		
1989			16 Jan–20 Jan	22 Dec–16 Jan	
1990			21 Dec–5 Jan	5 Jan–20 Jan	
1991	21 Dec–31 Dec	31 Dec–20 Jan			
1992				21 Dec–3 Jan	3 Jan–20 Jan
1993		21 Dec–26 Dec	26 Dec–20 Jan	20 Jan	
1994	21 Dec–7 Jan	7 Jan–20 Jan			
1995				21 Dec–15 Jan	15 Jan–20 Jan
1996		21 Dec–10 Jan	10 Jan–20 Jan		
1997				21 Dec–9 Jan	9 Jan–20 Jan
1998			21 Dec–4 Jan	4 Jan–20 Jan	
1999	21 Dec–31 Dec	31 Dec–20 Jan			
2000				21 Dec–3 Jan	3 Jan–20 Jan

The Capricorn Workbook

There are no right or wrong answers in this section. Its aim is to help you assess how you are doing with your life – in YOUR estimation – and to make the material of this book more personal and, I hope, more helpful for you.

1. The Capricorn in You
Which of the following Capricorn characteristics do you recognise in yourself?

ambitious	astute	committed
disciplined	hard-working	organising
patient	persevering	realistic
responsible	formal	tradition-loving

2. In which situations do you find yourself acting like this?

_____

_____

3. When you are feeling vulnerable, you may show some of the less constructive Capricorn traits. Do you recognise yourself in any of the following?

calculating	judgmental	depressing
cold	controlling	miserly

What kind of situations trigger off this behaviour and what do you think might help you, in these situations, to respond more positively?

_____

_____

4. You and Your Roles
a) Where, if anywhere, in your life do you play the role of Manager?

_____

_____

b) What, or whom, do you manage?

_____

_____

5. Do you play any of the following roles – in the literal or broad sense – in any part of your life? If not, would you like to? What might be your first step towards doing so?

Executive	Committee Member	President
Patriarch/Matriarch	Community Elder	Climber

_____

_____

6. Sun Aspects
If any of the following planets aspects your Sun, add each of the keywords for that planet to complete the following sentences. Which phrases ring true for you?

I am _____

My father is _____

My job requires that I am _____

Saturn Words (Use only if your Sun is aspected by Saturn)

ambitious	controlling	judgmental	mature
serious	strict	traditional	bureaucratic
cautious	committed	hard-working	disciplined
depressive	responsible	status-seeking	limiting

Uranus Words (Use only if your Sun is aspected by Uranus)

freedom-loving	progressive	rebellious	shocking
scientific	cutting-edge	detached	contrary
friendly	disruptive	eccentric	humanitarian
innovative	nonconformist	unconventional	exciting

Neptune Words (Use only if your Sun is aspected by Neptune)

sensitive	idealistic	artistic	impressionable
disappointing	impractical	escapist	self-sacrificing
spiritual	unrealistic	dreamy	glamorous
dependent	deceptive	rescuing	blissful

Pluto Words (Use only if your Sun is aspected by Pluto)

powerful	single-minded	intense	extreme
secretive	rotten	passionate	mysterious
investigative	uncompromising	ruthless	wealthy
abusive	regenerative	associated with sex, birth or death	

a) If one or more negative words describe you or your job, how might you turn that quality into something more positive or satisfying?

_____

_____

7. The Moon and You

Below are brief lists of what the Moon needs, in the various elements, to feel secure and satisfied. First find your Moon element, then estimate how much of each of the following you are expressing and receiving in your life, especially at home and in your relationships, on a scale of 0 to 5 where 0 = none and 5 = plenty.

FIRE MOONS — Aries, Leo, Sagittarius

attention	action	drama
recognition	self-expression	spontaneity
enthusiasm	adventure	leadership

EARTH MOONS — Taurus, Virgo, Capricorn

stability	orderly routine	sensual pleasures
material security	a sense of rootedness	control over your home life
regular body care	practical achievements	pleasurable practical tasks

AIR MOONS — Gemini, Libra, Aquarius

mental rapport	stimulating ideas	emotional space
friendship	social justice	interesting conversations
fairness	socialising	freedom to circulate

WATER MOONS — Cancer, Scorpio, Pisces

intimacy	a sense of belonging	emotional rapport
emotional safety	respect for your feelings	time and space to retreat
acceptance	cherishing and being cherished	warmth and comfort

a) Do you feel your Moon is being 'fed' enough?

yes _____ no _____

b) How might you satisfy your Moon needs even better?

_____

_____

8. You and Your Mercury

As a Capricorn, your Mercury can only be in Sagittarius, Capricorn or Aquarius. Below are some of the ways and situations in which Mercury in each of the elements might learn and communicate effectively. First find your Mercury sign, then circle the words you think apply to you.

Mercury in Fire (Sagittarius)

action	imagination	identifying with the subject matter
excitement	drama	playing with possibilities

Mercury in Earth (Capricorn)

time-tested methods	useful facts	well-structured information
'how to' instructions	demonstrations	hands on experience

Mercury in Air (Aquarius)

facts in categories	logic	demonstrable connections
rational arguments	theories	debate and sharing of ideas

Mercury in Water (As a Capricorn you can never have Mercury in a water sign; the words are included here for completeness)

pictures and images	charged atmospheres	feeling-linked information
intuitive understanding	emotional rapport	being shown personally

a) This game with Mercury can be done with a friend or on your own. Skim through a magazine until you find a picture that interests you. Then describe the picture – to your friend, or in writing or on tape. Notice what you emphasise and the kind of words you use. Now try to describe it using the language and emphasis of each of the other Mercury modes. How easy did you find that? Identifying the preferred Mercury style of others and using that style yourself can lead to improved communication all round.

9. Your Venus Values

Below are lists of qualities and situations that your Venus sign might enjoy. Assess on a scale of 0 to 5 how much your Venus desires and pleasures are met and expressed in your life. 0 = not at all, 5 = fully.

Venus in Scorpio

You will activate your Venus through anything that allows you to penetrate to the heart of life's mysteries, for example:

survival situations	money, power and sex	investigating secrets
transformative experiences	recycling	intense relationships

Venus in Sagittarius

You will activate your Venus through following your adventurous spirit, opening up new frontiers and sharing your enthusiasm with others, for example:

travelling	sport	searching for the meaning of life
teaching or preaching	inspiring others	publishing or broadcasting

Venus in Capricorn

You will activate your Venus through anything that makes you feel a respected member of the community, for example:

doing your duty	upholding tradition	working towards goals
achieving ambitions	heading a dynasty	acquiring social status

Venus in Aquarius

You will activate your Venus through freedom from the restraints of convention, for example:

sharing progressive ideas	unusual relationships	being nonconformist
humanitarian projects	teamwork	eccentric fashions

Venus in Pisces

You will activate your Venus through anything that allows you to experience fusion with something greater than yourself, for example:

relieving suffering	daydreaming	creating a glamorous image
spiritual devotion	voluntary service	losing yourself in art, music or love

a) How, and where, might you have more fun and pleasure by bringing more of what your Venus sign loves into your life?

_____

_____

b) Make a note here of the kind of gifts your Venus sign would love to receive. Then go on and spoil yourself . . .

_____

_____

Resources

Finding an Astrologer

I'm often asked what is the best way to find a reputable astrologer. Personal recommendation by someone whose judgement you trust is by far the best way. Ideally, the astrologer should also be endorsed by a reputable organisation whose members adhere to a strict code of ethics, which guarantees confidentiality and professional conduct.

Contact Addresses

Association of Professional Astrologers
www.professionalastrologers.org

APA members adhere to a strict code of professional ethics.

Astrological Association of Great Britain
www.astrologicalassociation.co.uk

The main body for astrology in the UK that also has information on astrological events and organisations throughout the world.

Faculty of Astrological Studies
www.astrology.org.uk

The teaching body internationally recognised for excellence in astrological education at all levels.

Your Capricorn Friends

You can keep a record of Capricorns you know here, with the page numbers of where to find their descriptions handy for future reference.

Name _____ Date of Birth _____

Aspects*	None	Saturn	Uranus	Neptune	Pluto
Moon Sign _____				p _____	
Mercury Sign _____				p _____	
Venus Sign _____				p _____	

Name _____ Date of Birth _____

Aspects*	None	Saturn	Uranus	Neptune	Pluto
Moon Sign _____				p _____	
Mercury Sign _____				p _____	
Venus Sign _____				p _____	

Name _____ Date of Birth _____

Aspects*	None	Saturn	Uranus	Neptune	Pluto
Moon Sign _____				p _____	
Mercury Sign _____				p _____	
Venus Sign _____				p _____	

Name _____ Date of Birth _____

Aspects*	None	Saturn	Uranus	Neptune	Pluto
Moon Sign _____				p _____	
Mercury Sign _____				p _____	
Venus Sign _____				p _____	

* Circle where applicable

Sign Summaries

SIGN	GLYPH	APPROX DATES	SYMBOL	ROLE	ELEMENT	QUALITY	PLANET	GLYPH	KEYWORD
1. Aries	♈	21/3 – 19/4	Ram	Hero	Fire	Cardinal	Mars	♂	Assertiveness
2. Taurus	♉	20/4 – 20/5	Bull	Steward	Earth	Fixed	Venus	♀	Stability
3. Gemini	♊	21/5 – 21/6	Twins	Go-Between	Air	Mutable	Mercury	☿	Communication
4. Cancer	♋	22/6 – 22/7	Crab	Caretaker	Water	Cardinal	Moon	☽	Nurture
5. Leo	♌	23/7 – 22/8	Lion	Performer	Fire	Fixed	Sun	☉	Glory
6. Virgo	♍	23/8 – 22/9	Maiden	Craftworker	Earth	Mutable	Mercury	☿	Skill
7. Libra	♎	23/9 – 22/10	Scales	Architect	Air	Cardinal	Venus	♀	Balance
8. Scorpio	♏	23/10 – 23/11	Scorpion	Survivor	Water	Fixed	Pluto	♇	Transformation
9. Sagittarius	♐	22/11 – 21/12	Archer	Adventurer	Fire	Mutable	Jupiter	♃	Wisdom
10. Capricorn	♑	22/12 – 19/1	Goat	Manager	Earth	Cardinal	Saturn	♄	Responsibility
11. Aquarius	♒	20/1 – 19/2	Waterbearer	Scientist	Air	Fixed	Uranus	♅	Progress
12. Pisces	♓	20/2 – 20/3	Fishes	Dreamer	Water	Mutable	Neptune	♆	Universality